An Introduction to the Science of Hadith

An Introduction to the Science of Hadith

Second Edition with Supplement

Suhaib Hasan

Al-Quran Society   جمعية القرآن

Contents

Foreword 9

Section A: Introduction 13

  A Brief History of *Mustalah al-Hadith* (Classification Of Hadith) 14

  Mustalah al-Hadith (Classification Of Hadith) 17

  Rijal al-Hadith (The Study Of The Reporters Of Hadith)................................. 18

Section B: The Classification of Hadith... 21

  1) According to the Reference to a Particular Authority 21

    Marfu'... 21

    Mauquf 21

    Maqtu'..22

  2) According to the Links in the Isnad..23

    Musnad..23

    Mursal, Munqati', Mu'dal, & Mu'allaq 24

    Authenticity of the *Mursal* Hadith 26

  3) According to the Number of Reporters Involved in Each Stage of the Isnad 33

    Mutawatir & Ahad..33

    Gharib, 'Aziz & Mashhur..35

  4) According to the Manner in Which the Hadith is Reported.................37

    Mudallas Hadith & *Tadlis* 37

    Musalsal 39

  5) According to the Nature of the Text and *Isnad* 40

    Shadhdh & Munkar.. 40

    Mudraj 42

6) According to a Hidden Defect Found in the *Isnad* or Text of a Hadith 43

Mudtarib 44

Maqlub...45

Ma'lul Or *Mu'allal*... 46

7) According to the Reliability and Memory of the Reporters 48

Sahih 49

Hasan 51

Several Weak *Ahadith* May Mutually Support Each Other to the Level of *Hasan* 53

Da'if 54

Maudu'...54

Section C: Further Branches of *Mustalah* and *Rijal al-Hadith* 57

Appendix: Verdicts on the *Ahadith* Mentioned in the Foreword....................61

Supplement to *An Introduction to the Science of Hadith* 71

Part One

The Knowledge of Hadith Mainly Covers Two Branches 72

1. Knowledge About a Companion 73

2. Discussion About Receiving the Hadith (*Tahammul*) and Imparting it (*Ada'*) 75

3. Scrutinizing the Authenticity of Hadith Among the Companions................ 76

4. The Knowledge About a Successor 78

5. Pre-Requisite for a *Sahih* Hadith.. 79

6. Continuity of *Isnad*.. 81

7. To Know the Hidden Cause (*'Illah*).. 84

8. *Shudhudh* (Oddness) in the Hadith 86

9. The Knowledge of *al-Jarh wa 'l-Ta'dil* (Disparaging And Authenticating)...87

10. Anthenticating Remarks.. 92

11. Disparaging Remarks... 94

12. What About a Person who Attracted Both Authenticating and Disparaging Remarks?.. 98

13. The Methods Through Which Knowledge is Carried 101

Part Two

A) Classification Of Hadith in Accordance With the Attributes of the Reporters 106

1. *Al-Sabiq wa 'l-Lahiq* (The Foremost and the Runner Up) 106

2. The Knowledge of Brothers and Sisters Among the Reporters 106

3. *Al-Muhmal* (Unknown) and *al-Mubham* (Obscure)...........................107

4. *Al-Musalsal* (Uniformly Linked) 108

5. *Al-Muttafiq wa 'l-Muftariq* (Common Names With Different Identities) ...108

6. *Al-Mu'talif wa 'l-Mukhtalif* (Similar but Pronounced Differently) 109

7. *Al-Mutashabih* المتشابه (Symmetrical) 109

8. *Al-Muharraf* (Interpolated) and *al-Musahhaf* (Distorted) 110

B) Classification Of Hadith In Accordance With the Age Group of the Reporters 111

1. The Narratives of *al-Aqran* (Contemporaries) and *Mudabbaj* (Beautified) .....
....111

2. Fathers Reporting From Sons 111

3. Sons Reporting From Their Fathers...112

4. Elders Reporting From Their Juniors...113

5. The Knowledge of the Life History of the Reporters 113

C) The Manners Required in Traditionists and Their Students.................114

A) The Manners Required by the Seekers of Knowledge...........................114

B) Manners Required in a Traditionist..115

C) Manners Related to the Court (*Majlis*) of Narrating Hadith...........116

D) Classification Of Hadith as Related to the Identity of the Reporters.......
....117

1. The Knowledge of Obscure Reporters (*Mubham*) 117

2. The Knowledge of Single Reports (*Al-Wuhdan*)..................................117

3. The Knowledge of Reporters With Different Names, as Well as Such Names Which are Either Unique in Their Structure or are Single Ones From Among the Reporters 118

4. Unique Nicknames (*Kunya*)..119

5. The Knowledge of Bynames or Titles (*Alqab*) 120

6. Those Attributed to Other Than Their Fathers...........................121

7. Attribution Contrary to What it Seems To Be 123

E) The Knowledge of Tabaqat (Groups) of the Reporters 123

F) The Knowledge of *Mawali* (Pl. *Maula*)...................................124

G) The Knowledge Related to the Hometowns of the Reporters 125

H) The Knowledge of *Mukhadram*...125

I) The Knowledge of Trustworthy Reporters who Were Held as Weak..126

J) The Knowledge of The Reporters of the Six Books.......................127

K) Other Branches of Knowledge 128

My Personal Ijazah 129

List if Hadith Terminology 131

FOREWORD

All Praise be to Allah, Lord of the Worlds. Peace and blessings of Allah be upon our Prophet Muhammad, and on his family and companions.

﴿ إِنَّا نَحْنُ نَزَّلْنَا ٱلذِّكْرَ وَإِنَّا لَهُۥ لَحَٰفِظُونَ ﴾

"We have undoubtedly sent down the Reminder, and We will truly preserve it." (Al-Qur'an, Surah al-Hijr, 15:9)

The above promise made by Allah is obviously fulfilled in the undisputed purity of the Qur'anic text throughout the fourteen centuries since its revelation. However, what is often forgotten by many Muslims is that the above divine promise also includes, by necessity, the Sunnah of the Prophet Muhammad ﷺ, for it is the practical example of the implementation of the Qur'anic guidance, the Wisdom taught to the Prophet ﷺ along with the Scripture, and neither the Qur'an nor the Sunnah can be understood correctly without recourse to the other.

Hence, Allah preserved the Qur'an from being initially lost by the martyrdom of its memorisers, by guiding the Rightly-Guided Caliphs, endorsed by the consensus of the Messenger's Companions ﷺ, to compile the *ayat* (signs, miracles, "verses") of the Qur'an into one volume, after these had been scattered in writing on various materials and in memory amongst many faithful hearts. He safeguarded it from corruption by its enemies: disbelievers, heretics, and false prophets, by enabling millions of believers to commit it to memory with ease. He protected its teachings by causing thousands of people of knowledge to learn from its deep treasures and convey them to the masses, and by sending renewers of His *Deen* at the beginning of every century.

Similarly, Allah preserved the Sunnah by enabling the Companions and those after them ﷺ to memorise, write down and pass on the statements of the Messenger ﷺ and the descriptions of his Way, as well as to continue the blessings of practising the Sunnah. Later, as the purity of the knowledge of the Sunnah became threatened, Allah caused the Muslim nation to produce outstanding individuals of incredible memory-skills and analytical expertise, who journeyed tirelessly to collect hundreds of thousands of narrations and distinguish the true words of precious wisdom of their Messenger ﷺ from those corrupted by weak memories, from forgeries by unscrupulous liars, and from the statements of the enormous number of *'ulama'*, the Companions and those who followed their way, who had taught in various centres of learning and helped to transmit the legacy of Muhammad ﷺ - all of this achieved through precise attention to the words narrated and detailed familiarity with the biographies of the thousands of reporters of Hadith. Action being the best way to preserve teachings, the renewers of Islam also revived the practice of the blessed authentic Sunnah.

Unfortunately however, statements will continue to be attributed to the Prophet ﷺ although the person quoting them may have no idea what the people of knowledge of Hadith have ruled regarding those *Ahadith*, thus ironically being in danger of contravening the Prophet's widely-narrated stern warnings about attributing incorrect/unsound statements to him. For example, here are some very commonly-quoted *Ahadith*, which actually vary tremendously in their degree of authenticity from the Prophet ﷺ:

1. "*Surah al-Ikhlas* is worth a third of the Qur'an."
2. The Hadith about the Ninety-Name Names of Allah.
3. Allah says, "I was a hidden treasure, and I wished to be known, so I created a creation (mankind), then made Myself known to them, and they recognised Me."

4.   Allah says, "Were it not for you (O Muhammad), I would not have created the universe."

5.   When Allah completed creation, He wrote in a Book (which is) with Him, above His Throne, "Verily, My Mercy will prevail over My Wrath."

6.   Allah says, "Neither My heaven nor My earth can contain Me, but the heart of My believing slave can contain Me."

7.   "He who knows himself, knows his Lord."

8.   "Where is Allah?"

9.   "Love of one's homeland is part of Faith."

10.   "I have left amongst you two things which, if you hold fast to them, you will never stray: the Book of Allah, and my Sunnah."

11.   "I have left among you that which if you abide by, you will never go astray: the Book of Allah, and my Family, the Members of my House."

12.   The Hadith giving ten Companions, by name, the good tidings of Paradise.

13.   "If the *iman* (faith) of Abu Bakr was weighed against the *iman* of all the people of the earth, the former would outweigh the latter."

14.   "I am the City of Knowledge, and 'Ali is its Gate."

15.   "My companions are like the stars: whichever of them you follow, you will be guided."

16.   "The differing amongst my *Ummah* is a mercy."

17.   "My *Ummah* will split up into seventy-three sects: seventy-two will be in the Fire, and one in the Garden."

18.   Prophecies about the coming of the Mahdi (the guided one), Dajjal (the False Christ, the Anti-Christ) and the return of Jesus Christ son of Mary.

19.   Description of punishment and bliss in the grave, for the wicked and pious people respectively.

20.   Intercession by the Prophet ﷺ, and the believers seeing Allah, on the Day of Judgment.

21. "Paradise is under the feet of mothers."

22. "Paradise is under the shade of swords."

23. "Seeking knowledge is a duty upon every Muslim."

24. "Seek knowledge, even if you have to go to China."

25. "The ink of the scholar is holier than the blood of the martyr."

26. "We have returned from the lesser Jihad to the greater Jihad (i.e. the struggle against the evil of one's soul)."

The methodology of the expert scholars of Hadith in assessing such narrations and sorting out the genuine from the mistaken/fabricated etc., forms the subject-matter of a wealth of material left to us by the *muhaddithun* (scholars of Hadith, "traditionists"). This short treatise is a humble effort to introduce this extremely wide subject to English readers. The author has derived great benefit from the outstanding scholarly work in this field, *Muqaddimah Ibn al-Salah*.

A brief explanation of the verdicts from the experts in this field on the above *Ahadith* is given in the Appendix.

We ask Allah to accept this work, and make it beneficial to its readers.

SECTION A:
INTRODUCTION

The Muslims are agreed that the Sunnah of the Prophet Muhammad ﷺ is the second of the two revealed fundamental sources of Islam, after the Glorious Qur'an. The authentic Sunnah is contained within the vast body of Hadith literature.[1]

A Hadith (pl. *Ahadith*) is composed of two parts: the *matn* (text) and the *isnad* (chain of reporters). A text may seem to be logical and reasonable but it needs an authentic *isnad* with reliable reporters to be acceptable; 'Abdullah b. al-Mubarak (d. 181 AH), one of the illustrious teachers of Imam al-Bukhari, said,

» الاسناد من الدين ولو الإسناد لقال من شاء ما شاء «

> "The *isnad* is part of the religion: had it not been for the *isnad*,
> whoever wished to would have said whatever he liked."[2]

During the lifetime of the Prophet ﷺ and after his death, his Companions (*Sahabah*) used to refer to him directly, when quoting his sayings. The

---

[1] Ar. Sunnah: Way, Path, Tradition, Example. See *An Introduction to the Sunnah* by Suhaib Hasan (Understanding Islam Series no. 5, published by Al-Quran Society), for Qur'anic proofs of revelation besides the Qur'an, the importance of the Sunnah, and a brief history of the collections of Hadith. See also Imam al- Shafi'i's *al-Risalah* for the authoritative position of the Sunnah (Eng. trans., pp. 109- 116).

[2] Related by Imam Muslim in the Introduction to his Sahih - see *Sahih* Muslim (ed. M.F. 'Abdul Baqi, 5 vols., Cairo, 1374/1955), 1:15 & *Sahih Muslim bi Sharh an-Nawawi* (18 vols. in 6, Cairo, 1349), 1:87. The existing English translation of Sahih Muslim, by Abdul Hamid Siddiqi, does not contain this extremely valuable Introduction.

Successors (*Tabi'un*) followed suit; some of them used to quote the Prophet ﷺ through the Companions while others would omit the intermediate authority - such a Hadith was later known as *mursal*. It was found that the missing link between the Successor and the Prophet ﷺ might be one person, i.e. a Companion, or two people, the extra person being an older Successor who heard the Hadith from the Companion. This is an example of how the need for the verification of each *isnad* arose; Imam Malik (d. 179) said, "The first one to utilise the *isnad* was Ibn Shihab al- Zuhri" (d. 124). [3]

The other more important reason was the deliberate fabrication of *Ahadith* by various sects which appeared amongst the Muslims, in order to support their views (see later, under discussion of *maudu' Ahadith*). Ibn Sirin (d. 110), a Successor, said, "They would not ask about the *isnad*. But when the *fitnah* (trouble, turmoil, esp. civil war) happened, they said: Name to us your men. So the narrations of the *Ahl al-Sunnah* (Adherents to the Sunnah) would be accepted, while those of the *Ahl al-Bid'ah* (Adherents to Innovation) would not be accepted."[4]

A Brief History of *Mustalah al-Hadith* (Classification of Hadith)

As time passed, more reporters were involved in each *isnad*, and so the situation demanded strict discipline in the acceptance of *Ahadith*; the rules regulating this discipline are known as *Mustalah al-Hadith* (the Classification of Hadith).

Amongst the early traditionists (*muhaddithin*, scholars of Hadith), the rules and criteria governing their study of Hadith were meticulous but some of their terminology varied from person to person, and their principles began

---

[3] Ibn Abi Hatim al-Razi, *Al-Jarh wa l-Ta'dil* (8 vols., Hyderabad, 1360-1373), 1:20.

[4] *Sahih* Muslim, 1:15. See Suhaib Hasan, *Criticism of Hadith among Muslims with reference to Sunan Ibn Maja* (Ta Ha publishers / Al-Quran Society, London, 1407/1986), pp. 15-17 for discussion of this statement of Ibn Sirin.

to be systematically written down, but scattered amongst various books, e.g. in *Al-Risalah* of al- Shafi'i (d. 204), the Introduction to the *Sahih* of Muslim (d. 261) and the *Jami'* of al-Tirmidhi (d. 279); many of the criteria of early traditionists, e.g. al-Bukhari, were deduced by later scholars from a careful study of which reporters or *isnads* were accepted and rejected by them.

One of the earliest writings to attempt to cover *Mustalah* comprehensively, using standard (i.e. generally-accepted) terminology, was the work by al-Ramahurmuzi (d. 360). The next major contribution was *Ma'rifah 'Ulum al-Hadith* by al- Hakim (d. 405), which covered fifty classifications of Hadith, but still left some points untouched; Abu Nu'aim al-Isbahani (d. 430) completed some of the missing parts to this work. After that came *Al-Kifayah fi 'Ilm al- Riwayah* of al-Khatib al-Baghdadi (d. 463) and another work on the manner of teaching and studying Hadith; later scholars were considered to be greatly indebted to al-Khatib's work.

After further contributions by Qadi 'Iyad al-Yahsubi (d. 544) and Abu Hafs al-Mayanji (d. 580) among others, came the work which, although modest in size, was so comprehensive in its excellent treatment of the subject that it came to be the standard reference for thousands of scholars and students of Hadith to come, over many centuries until the present day: *'Ulum al-Hadith* of Abu 'Amr 'Uthman Ibn al-Salah (d. 643), commonly known as *Muqaddimah Ibn al-Salah*, compiled while he taught in the Dar al-Hadith of several cities in Syria. Some of the numerous later works based on that of Ibn al-Salah are:

- An abridgement of *Muqaddimah*, *Al-Irshad* by al- Nawawi (d. 676), which he later summarised in his *Taqrib*; al-Suyuti (d. 911) compiled a valuable commentary on the latter entitled *Tadrib al-Rawi*.
- *Ikhtisar 'Ulum al-Hadith* of Ibn Kathir (d. 774), *Al-Khulasah* of al-Tibi (d. 743), *Al-Minhal* of Badr al-Din b. Jama'ah (d. 733), *Al-*

Muqni' of Ibn al-Mulaqqin (d. 802) and *Mahasin al-Istilah* of al-Bulqini (d. 805), all of which are abridgements of *Muqaddimah Ibn al- Salah.*

- *Al-Nukat* of al-Zarkashi (d. 794), *Al-Taqyid wa 'l-Idah* of al-'Iraqi (d. 806) and *Al-Nukat* of Ibn Hajar al-'Asqalani (d. 852), all of which are further notes on the points made by Ibn al-Salah.

- *Alfiyyah al-Hadith* of al-'Iraqi, a rewriting of *Muqaddimah* in the form of a lengthy poem, which became the subject of several commentaries, including two (one long, one short) by the author himself, *Fath al-Mughith* of al-Sakhawi (d. 903), *Qatar al-Durar* of al-Suyuti and *Fath al-Baqi* of Shaykh Zakariyyah al-Ansari (d. 928).

Other notable treatises on *Mustalah* include:

- *Al-Iqtirah* of Ibn Daqiq al-'Id (d. 702).
- *Tanqih al-Anzar* of Muhammad b. Ibrahim al- Wazir (d. 840), the subject of a commentary by al-Amir al-San'ani (d. 1182).
- *Nukhbah al-Fikar* of Ibn Hajar al-'Asqalani, again the subject of several commentaries, including one by the author himself, one by his son Muhammad, and those of 'Ali al-Qari (d. 1014), 'Abd al-Ra'uf al-Munawi (d. 1031) and Muhammad b. 'Abd al-Hadi al-Sindi (d. 1138). Among those who rephrased the *Nukhbah* in poetic form are al-Tufi (d. 893) and al-Amir al-San'ani.
- *Alfiyyah al-Hadith* of al-Suyuti, the most comprehensive poetic work in the field.
- *Al-Manzumah* of al-Baiquni, which was expanded upon by, amongst others, al-Zurqani (d. 1122) and Nawab Siddiq Hasan Khan (d. 1307).
- *Qawa'id al-Tahdith* of Jamal al-Din al-Qasimi (d. 1332).
- *Taujih al-Nazar* of Tahir al-Jaza'iri (d. 1338), a summary of al-Hakim's *Ma'rifah.*

Mustalah al-Hadith (Classification of Hadith)

Mustalah books speak of a number of classes of Hadith in accordance with their status. The following broad classifications can be made, each of which is explained in the later sections:

- According to the reference to a particular authority, e.g. the Prophet ﷺ, a Companion, or a Successor; such *Ahadith* are called *marfu'* (elevated), *mauquf* (stopped) and *maqtu'* (severed) respectively.

- According to the links in the *isnad*, i.e. whether the chain of reporters is interrupted or uninterrupted, e.g. *musnad* (supported), *muttasil* (continuous), *munqati'* (broken), *mu'allaq* (hanging), *mu'dal* (perplexing) and *mursal* (hurried).

- According to the number of reporters involved in each stage of the *isnad*, e.g. *mutawatir* (consecutive) and *ahad* (isolated), the latter being divided into *gharib* (scarce, strange), *'aziz* (rare, strong), and *mashhur* (famous).

- According to the manner in which the Hadith has been reported, such as using the (Arabic) words 'an (عن "on the authority of"), *haddathana* (حدثنا "he narrated to us"), *akhbarana* (أخبرنا "he informed us") or *sami'tu* (سمعت "I heard"). In this category falls the discussion about *mudallas* (concealed) and *musalsal* (uniformly-linked) *Ahadith*.[5]

- According to the nature of the *matn* and *isnad*, e.g. an addition by a reliable reporter, known as *ziyadatu thiqah*, or opposition by a lesser authority to a more reliable one, known as *shadhdh* (irregular). In some cases, a text containing a vulgar expression,

---

[5] [Note: In the quotation of *isnads* in the remainder of this book, the first mode of narration mentioned above will be represented with a single broken line thus: ---. The three remaining modes of narration mentioned above, which all strongly indicate a clear, direct transmission of the Hadith, are represented by a double line thus: ===.]

unreasonable remark or obviously-erroneous statement is rejected by the traditionists outright without consideration of the isnad: such a Hadith is known as *munkar* (denounced). If an expression or statement is proved to be an addition by a reporter to the text, it is declared as *mudraj* (interpolated).

- According to a hidden defect found in *the* isnad or text of a Hadith. Although this could be included in some of the previous categories, a Hadith *mu'allal* (defective Hadith) is worthy to be explained separately. The defect can be caused in many ways; e.g. two types of Hadith *mu'allal* are known as *maqlub* (overturned) and *mudtarib* (shaky).

- According to the reliability and memory of the reporters; the final judgment on a Hadith depends crucially on this factor: verdicts such as *sahih* (sound), *hasan* (good), *da'if* (weak) and *maudu'* (fabricated, forged) rest mainly upon the nature of the reporters in the *isnad*.

Rijal al-Hadith (the Study of the Reporters of Hadith)

Mustalah al-Hadith is strongly associated with *Rijal al-Hadith* (the study of the reporters of Hadith). In scrutinising the reporters of a Hadith, authenticating or disparaging remarks made by recognised experts, from amongst the Successors and those after them, were found to be of great help. Examples of such remarks, in descending order of authentication, are:

- "Imam (leader), Hafiz (preserver)."
- "Reliable, trustworthy."
- "Makes mistakes."
- "Weak."
- "Abandoned (by the traditionists)."

- "Liar, used to fabricate *Ahadith*."[6]

Reporters who have been unanimously described by statements such as the first two may contribute to a *sahih* ("sound", see later) *isnad*. An *isnad* containing a reporter who is described by the last two statements is likely to be *da'if jiddan* (very weak) or *maudu'* (fabricated). Reporters who are the subject of statements such as the middle two above will cause the *isnad* to be *da'if* (weak), although several of them relating the same Hadith independently will often increase the rank of the Hadith to the level of *hasan* (good). If the remarks about a particular reporter conflict, a careful verdict has to be arrived at after in-depth analysis of e.g. the reason given for any disparagement, the weight of each type of criticism, the relative strictness or leniency of each critic, etc.

The earliest remarks cited in the books of *Rijal* go back to a host of Successors, followed by those after them until the period of the six canonical traditionists, a period covering the first three centuries of Islam. A list of such names is provided by the author in his thesis, Criticism of Hadith among Muslims with reference to *Sunan Ibn Majah*, at the end of chapters IV, V and VI.

Among the earliest available works in this field are *Tarikh* of Ibn Ma'in (d. 233), *Tabaqat* of Khalifa b. Khayyat (d. 240), *Tarikh* of al-Bukhari (d. 256), *Kitab al-Jarh wa 'l-Ta'dil* of Ibn Abi Hatim (d. 327) and *Tabaqat* of Muhammad b. Sa'd (d. 320).

A number of traditionists made efforts specifically for the gathering of information about the reporters of the five famous collections of Hadith, those of al-Bukhari (d. 256), Muslim (d. 261), Abu Dawud (d. 275), al-

---

[6] Remarks like these are exceptions from the basic Islamic prohibition of backbiting (ghibah) another Muslim, even if the statement is true. Such exceptions are allowed, even obligatory in some cases, where general benefit to the Muslim public is at stake, such as knowing which ahadith are authentic. See e.g. *Riyad al- Salihin* of al-Nawawi, Chapter on Backbiting, for the justification for certain types of backbiting from the Qur'an and Sunnah.

Tirmidhi (d. 279) and al-Nasa'i (d. 303), giving authenticating and disparaging remarks in detail. The first major such work to include also the reporters of Ibn Majah (d. 273) is the ten-volume collection of al-Hafiz 'Abd al-Ghani al-Maqdisi (d. 600), known as *Al-Kamal fi Asma' al-Rijal*. Later, Jamal al-Din Abu 'l-Hajjaj Yusuf b. 'Abd al-Rahman al-Mizzi (d. 742) prepared an edited and abridged version of this work, punctuated by places and countries of origin of the reporters; he named it *Tahdhib al- Kamal fi Asma' al-Rijal* and produced it in twelve volumes. Further, one of al-Mizzi's gifted pupils, Shams al-Din Abu 'Abdullah Muhammad b. Ahmad b. 'Uthman b. Qa'imaz al- Dhahabi (d. 748), summarised his shaikh's work and produced two abridgements: a longer one called *Tadhhib al-Tahdhib* and a shorter one called *Al-Kashif fi Asma' Rijal al-Kutub al-Sittah*.

A similar effort with the work of al-Mizzi was made by Ibn Hajar (d. 852), who prepared a lengthy but abridged version, with about one- third of the original omitted, entitled *Tahdhib al-Tahdhib* in twelve shorter volumes. Later, he abridged this further to a relatively-humble two- volume work called *Taqrib al-Tahdhib*.

The work of al-Dhahabi was not left unedited; al-Khazraji (Safi al-Din Ahmad b. 'Abdullah, d. after 923) summarised it and also made valuable additions, producing his *Khulasah*.

A number of similar works deal with either trustworthy reporters only, e.g. *Kitab al-Thiqat* by al-'Ijli (d. 261) and *Tadhkirah al-Huffaz* by al-Dhahabi, or with disparaged authorities only, e.g. *Kitab al-Du'afa' wa al-Matrukin* by al-Nasa'i and *Kitab al-Majruhin* by Muhammad b. Hibban al-Busti (d. 354).

Two more works in this field which include a large number of reporters, both authenticated and disparaged, are *Mizan al-I'tidal* of al-Dhahabi and *Lisan al-Mizan* of Ibn Hajar.

SECTION B: THE CLASSIFICATION OF HADITH

1) ACCORDING TO THE REFERENCE TO A PARTICULAR AUTHORITY

The following principal types of Hadith are important:

Marfu' (مرفوع) "elevated": A narration from the Prophet ﷺ, e.g. a reporter (whether a Companion, Successor or other) says, "The Messenger of Allah said ..." For example, the very first Hadith in *Sahih al-Bukhari* is as follows: Al- Bukhari === Al-Humaidi 'Abdullah b. al-Zubair === Sufyan === Yahya b. Sa'id al-Ansari === Muhammad b. Ibrahim al-Taymi === 'Alqamah b. Waqqas al-Laithi, who said: I heard 'Umar b. al- Khattab saying, while on the pulpit, "I heard Allah's Messenger ﷺ saying: The reward of deeds depends on the intentions, and every person will get the reward according to what he has intended; so whoever emigrated for wordly benefits or for a woman to marry, his emigration was for what he migrated."

Mauquf (موقوف) "stopped": A narration from a Companion only, i.e. his own statement; e.g. al-Bukhari reports in his *Sahih*, in *Kitab al-Fara'id* (Book of the Laws of Inheritance), that Abu Bakr, Ibn 'Abbas and Ibn al-Zubair said, "The grandfather is (treated like) a father."

It should be noted that certain expressions used by a Companion generally render a Hadith to be considered as being effectively *marfu'* although it is *mauquf* on the face of it, e.g. the following:

- "We were commanded to ..."
- "We were forbidden from ..."
- "We used to do ..."
- "We used to say/do ... while the Messenger of Allah was amongst us."
- "We did not use to mind such-and-such..."
- "It used to be said ..."
- "It is from the Sunnah to ..."
- "It was revealed in the following circumstances: ..." speaking about a verse of the Qur'an.

Maqtu' (مقطوع) "severed": A narration from a Successor, e.g. Muslim reports in the Introduction to his *Sahih* that Ibn Sirin (d. 110) said, "This knowledge (i.e. Hadith) is the Religion, so be careful from whom you take your religion."

The authenticity of each of the above three types of Hadith depends on other factors such as the reliability of its reporters, the nature of the linkage amongst them, etc. However, the above classification is extremely useful, since through it the sayings of the Prophet ﷺ can be distinguished at once from those of Companions or Successors; this is especially helpful in debate about matters of *Fiqh*.

Imam Malik's *Al-Muwatta'*, one of the early collections of Hadith, contains a relatively even ratio of these types of Hadith, as well as *mursal Ahadith* (which are discussed later). According to Abu Bakr al-Abhari (d. 375), *Al-Muwatta'* contains the following:

- 600 *marfu' Ahadith*,
- 613 *mauquf Ahadith*,
- 285 *maqtu' Ahadith*, and

- 28 *mursal Ahadith*; a total of 1726 *Ahadith*.[7]

Among other collections, relatively more *mauquf* and *maqtu' Ahadith* are found in *Al-Musannaf* of Ibn Abi Shaibah (d. 235), *Al-Musannaf* of 'Abd al-Razzaq (d. 211) and the *Tafsirs* of Ibn Jarir (d. 310), Ibn Abi Hatim (d. 327) and Ibn al-Mundhir (d. 319).[8]

2) ACCORDING TO THE LINKS IN THE ISNAD

Musnad (مسند)

Al-Hakim defines a *musnad* ("supported") Hadith as follows:

> "A Hadith which a traditionist reports from his *shaykh* from whom he is known to have heard (*Ahadith*) at a time of life suitable for learning, and similarly in turn for each *shaykh*, until the *isnad* reaches a well- known Companion, who in turn reports from the Prophet ﷺ."[9]

By this definition, an ordinary *muttasil* Hadith (i.e. one with an uninterrupted *isnad*) is excluded if it goes back only to a Companion or Successor, as is a *marfu'* Hadith which has an interrupted *isnad*.

Al-Hakim gives the following example of a *musnad* Hadith:

> We reported from Abu 'Amr 'Uthman b. Ahmad al-Sammak al-Baghdadi === Al-Hasan b. Mukarram === 'Uthman b. 'Amr === Yunus --- al-Zuhri --- 'Abdullah b. Ka'b b. Malik --- his

---

[7] Muhammad Adib Salih, *Lamahat fi Usul al-Hadith* (2nd ed., al-Maktab al-Islami, Beirut, 1389), p. 143.

[8] Tahir b. Ahmad al-Jaza'iri, *Taujih al-Nazar ila Usul al-Nazar* (Maktaba 'Ilmiyyah, Madinah, N.D.), p. 68.

[9] Muhammad b. 'Abdullah al-Hakim, *Ma'rifah 'Ulum al-Hadith* (ed. Mu'azzam Husain, Cairo, 1937), p. 17.

father, who asked Ibn Abi Hadrad for payment of a debt he owed to him, in the mosque. During the ensuing argument, their voices were raised until heard by the Messenger of Allah ﷺ, who eventually lifted the curtain of his apartment and said, "O Ka'b! Write off a part of your debt" - he meant remission of half of it. So he agreed, and the man paid him.

He then remarks,

"Now, my hearing from Ibn al-Simak is well- known, as is his from Ibn Mukarram; al-Hasan's link with 'Uthman b. 'Amr and the latter's with Yunus b. Zaid are known as well; Yunus is always remembered with al-Zuhri, and the latter with the sons of Ka'b b. Malik, whose link to their father and his companionship of the Prophet ﷺ are well- established."[10]

The term *musnad* is also applied to those collections of *Ahadith* which give the *Ahadith* of each Companion separately. Among the early compilers of such a *Musnad* were Yahya b. 'Abd al- Hamid al-Himmani (d. 228) at Kufah and Musaddad b. Musarhad (d. 228) at Basrah. The largest existing collection of *Ahadith* of Companions arranged in this manner is that of Imam Ahmad b. Hanbal (d. 241), which contains around thirty thousand *Ahadith*. Another larger work is attributed to the famous Andalusian traditionist Baqi b. Makhlad al-Qurtubi (d. 276), but unfortunately it is now untraceable.

Mursal (مرسل), *Munqati'* (منقطع), *Mu'dal* (معضل), & *Mu'allaq* (معلق)

If the link between the Successor and the Prophet ﷺ is missing, the Hadith is *mursal* ("hurried"), e.g. when a Successor says, "The Prophet said..."

---

[10] *Ibid.*

However, if a link anywhere before the Successor (i.e. closer to the traditionist recording the Hadith) is missing, the Hadith is *munqati'* ("broken"). This applies even if there is an apparent link, e.g. an *isnad* seems to be *muttasil* ("continuous") but one of the reporters is known to have never heard *Ahadith* from his immediate authority, even though he may be his contemporary. The term *munqati'* is also applied by some scholars to a narration such as where a reporter says, "a man narrated to me..." without naming this authority.[11]

If the number of consecutive missing reporters in the *isnad* exceeds one, the *isnad* is *mu'dal* ("perplexing"). If the reporter omits the whole *isnad* and quotes the Prophet ﷺ directly (i.e. the link is missing at the beginning, unlike the case with a *mursal isnad*), the Hadith is called *mu'allaq* ("hanging") - sometimes it is known as *balaghah* ("to reach"); for example, Imam Malik sometimes says in *Al-Muwatta'*, "It reached me that the Messenger of Allah ﷺ said ..."

Example of a *munqati'* Hadith:

> Al-Hakim reported from Muhammad b. Mus'ab === al-Auza'i -
> -- Shaddad Abu 'Ammar --- Umm al-Fadl bint al-Harith, who
> said: I came to the Messenger of Allah ﷺ and said, "I have seen
> in a vision last night as if a part of your body was cut out and
> placed in my lap." He said, "You have seen something good.
> Allah Willing, Fatimah will give birth to a lad who will be in
> your lap." After that, Fatimah gave birth to al-Husain, who
> used to be in my lap, in accordance with the statement of the
> Messenger of Allah ﷺ. One day, I came to the Messenger of
> Allah ﷺ and placed al-Husain in his lap. I noticed that both his
> eyes were shedding tears. He said, "Jibril came to me and told
> me that my Ummah will kill this son of mine, and he brought

---

[11] Jalal al-Din al-Suyuti, *Tadrib al-Rawi* (ed. A.A. Latif, 1st ed., Cairo, 1379/1959), 1:197.

me some of the reddish dust of that place (where he will be killed)."

Al-Hakim said, "This is a *sahih* Hadith according to the conditions of the *Two Shaykhs* (i.e. Bukhari & Muslim), but they did not collect it." Al-Dhahabi says, "No, the Hadith is *munqati'* and *da'if*, because Shaddad never met Umm al-Fadl and Muhammad b. Mus'ab is weak."[12]

Example of a *mu'dal* Hadith:

> Ibn Abi Hatim === Ja'far b. Ahmad b. al-Hakam Al- Qurashi in the year 254 === Sulaiman b. Mansur b. 'Ammar === 'Ali b. 'Asim --- Sa'id --- Qatadah --- Ubayy b. Ka'b, who reported that the Messenger of Allah ﷺ said, "After Adam had tasted from the tree, he ran away, but the tree caught his hair. It was proclaimed: 'O Adam! Are you running away from Me?' He said: 'No, but I feel ashamed before You.' He said: 'O Adam! Go away from My neighbourhood, for by My Honour, no-one who disobeys Me can live here near Me; even if I were to create people like you numbering enough to fill the earth and they were to disobey Me, I would make them live in a home of sinners.'"

Ibn Kathir remarks, "This is a *gharib* Hadith. There is *inqita'*, in fact *i'dal*, between Qatadah and Ubayy b. Ka'b ﷺ."[13]

Authenticity of the *Mursal* Hadith

There has been a great deal of discussion amongst the scholars regarding the authenticity of the *mursal* Hadith (pl. *marasil*), since it is quite probable

---

[12] Al-Dhahabi, *Talkhis al-Mustadrak* (printed with Mustadrak al-Hakim, 4 vols., Hyderabad), 3:176.

[13] Abu 'l-Fida' 'Imad al-Din Ibn Kathir, *Tafsir al-Qur'an al-Azim* (4 vols., Cairo, N.D.), 1:80.

that a Successor might have omitted two names, those of an elder Successor and a Companion, rather than just one name, that of a Companion.

If the Successor is known to have omitted the name of a Companion only, then the Hadith is held to be authentic, for a Successor can only report from the Prophet ﷺ through a Companion; the omission of the name of the Companion does not affect the authenticity of the *isnad* since all Companions are held to be trustworthy and reliable, by both Qur'anic injunctions and sayings of the Prophet ﷺ.

However, opinions vary in the case where the Successor might have omitted the names of two authorities (since not all the Successors were reliable in matters of Hadith). For example, two widely differing positions on this issue are:

(i) The *marasil* of elder Successors such as Sa'id b. al-Musayyab (d. 94) and 'Ata' b. Abi Rabah (d. 114) are acceptable because all their *marasil*, after investigation, are found to come through the Companions only. However, the *marasil* of younger Successors are only acceptable if the names of their immediate authorities are known through other sources; if not, they are rejected outright.

(ii) The *marasil* of Successors and those who report from them are acceptable without any investigation at all. This opinion is supported by the Kufi school of traditionists, but is severely attacked by the majority.

To be precise in this issue, let us investigate in detail the various opinions regarding the *mursal* Hadith:

1. The opinion held by Imam Malik and all Maliki jurists is that the *mursal* of a trustworthy person is valid as proof and as justification for a practice, just like a *musnad* Hadith.[14] This view has been developed to such an extreme that to some of them, the *mursal* is even better than the *musnad*, based on the following reasoning:

> "The one who reports a *musnad* Hadith leaves you with the names of the reporters for further investigation and scrutiny, whereas the one who narrates by way of *irsal*, being a knowledgeable and trustworthy person himself, has already done so and found the Hadith to be sound. In fact, he saves you from further research."[15]

2. Imam Abu Hanifah (d. 150) holds the same opinion as Malik; he accepts the *mursal* Hadith whether or not it is supported by another Hadith.[16]

3. Imam al-Shafi'i (d. 204) has discussed this issue in detail in his *al-Risalah*; he requires the following conditions to be met before accepting a *mursal* Hadith:

i. In the narrative, he requires that one of the following conditions be met:

    a. that it be reported also as *musnad* through another *isnad*;

    b. that its contents be reported as *mursal* through another reliable source with a different *isnad*;

    c. that the meaning be supported by the sayings of some Companions; or

    d. that most scholars hold the same opinion as conveyed by the *mursal* Hadith.

ii. Regarding the narrator, he requires that one of the following conditions be met:

    a. that he be an elder Successor;

---

[14] Yusuf b. 'Abdullah Ibn 'Abdul Barr, *Tajrid al- Tamhid lima fi l-Muwatta' min al-Asanid* (Cairo, 1350), 1:2.
[15] *Ibid.*
[16] Al-Suyuti, 1:198.

> b. that if he names the person missing in the *isnad* elsewhere, he does not usually name an unknown person or someone not suitable for reporting from acceptably; or that he does not contradict a reliable person when he happens to share with him in a narration.[17]

On the basis of these arguments, al-Shafi'i accepts the *irsal* of Sa'id b. al-Musayyab, one of the elder Successors. For example, al-Shafi'i considers the issue of selling meat in exchange for a living animal: he says that Malik told him, reporting from Zaid b. Aslam, who reported from Ibn al-Musayyab that the Messenger of Allah ﷺ forbade the selling of meat in exchange for an animal. He then says, "This is our opinion, for the *irsal* of Ibn al-Musayyib is fine."[18]

4. Imam Ahmad b. Hanbal (d. 241) accepts *mursal* and (other) *da'if* (weak) *Ahadith* if nothing opposing them is found regarding a particular issue, preferring them to *qiyas* (analogical deduction). By *da'if* here is meant *Ahadith* which are not severely weak, e.g. *batil, munkar,* or *maudu'*, since Imam Ahmad classified *Ahadith* into *sahih* and *da'if* rather than into *sahih, hasan* and *da'if*, the preference of most later traditionists. Hence, the category *da'if* in his view applied to *Ahadith* which were relatively close to being *sahih*, and included many *Ahadith* which were classed as *hasan* by other scholars.[19] Overlooking this fact has caused misunderstanding about Imam Ahmad's view on the place of *da'if Ahadith* in rulings of *Fiqh* and in matters of *Fada'il al-A'mal* (virtues of various acts of worship).

5. Ibn Hazm (d. 456) rejects the *mursal* Hadith outright; he says that the *mursal* is unacceptable, whether it comes through Sa'id b. al-Musayyib or

---

[17] For the discussion in detail, see al-Shafi'i, *al-Risalah* (ed. Ahmad Shakir, Cairo, 1358/1940, pp. 461-470; English translation: M. Khadduri, 2nd ed., Islamic Texts Society, Cambridge, 1987, pp. 279-284, where the *mursal* Hadith has been translated as "interrupted tradition").

[18] Al-Suyuti, 1:199; Muhammad b. Mustafa al-Ghadamsi, *Al-Mursal min al-Hadith* (Darif Ltd., London, N.D.), p.71.

[19] Ibn al-Qayyim, *I'lam al-Muwaqqi'in* (2nd ed., 4 vols. in 2, Dar al-Fikr, Beirut, 1397/1977), 1:31.

al-Hasan al-Basri. To him, even the *mursal* which comes through someone who was not well-known to be amongst the Companions would be unacceptable.[20]

6. Abu Dawud (d . 275) accepts the *mursal* under two conditions:

i. that no musnad Hadith is found regarding that issue;

ii. or that if a musnad Hadith is found, it is not contradicted by the mursal Hadith.[21]

7. Ibn Abi Hatim (d. 327) does not give a specific opinion about the *mursal* Hadith. However, he did collect an anthology of 469 reporters of Hadith, including four female reporters, whose narratives were subjected to criticism due to *irsal*. This collection is known as *Kitab al-Marasil.*

8. Al-Hakim (d. 405) is extremely reluctant to accept the *mursal* Hadith except in the case of elder Successors. He holds, on the basis of the Qur'an, that knowledge is based on what is heard (directly), not on what is reported (indirectly). In this regard, he quotes Yazid b. Harun who asked Hammad b. Laith: "O Abu Isma'il! Did Allah mention the *Ahl al-Hadith* (scholars of Hadith) in the Qur'an?" He replied, "Yes! Did you not hear the saying of Allah,

$$ \text{۞ وَمَا كَانَ ٱلْمُؤْمِنُونَ لِيَنفِرُواْ كَآفَّةً فَلَوْلَا نَفَرَ مِن كُلِّ فِرْقَةٍ مِّنْهُمْ طَآئِفَةٌ لِّيَتَفَقَّهُواْ فِى ٱلدِّينِ وَلِيُنذِرُواْ قَوْمَهُمْ إِذَا رَجَعُوٓاْ إِلَيْهِمْ لَعَلَّهُمْ يَحْذَرُونَ } $$

'If a party from every expedition remained behind, they[22] could devote themselves to studies in religion and admonish

---

[20] Ibn Hazm, *Al-Ihkam fi Usul al-Ahkam* (Matba'ah al-Sa'adah, Cairo, 1345), 2:135.

[21] Al-Hazimi, *Shurut al-A'immah al-Khamsah* (ed. M.Z. al-Kauthari, Cairo, N.D.), p. 45.

[22] According to the different interpretations of this verse, "they" here could refer to those who stay behind, or those who go forth.

> the people when they return to them, that thus they may
> guard themselves (against evil)' (Qur'an, 9:122).

This concerns those who set off to seek knowledge, and then return to those who remained behind in order to teach them."[23]

Al-Hakim then remarks, "This verse shows that the acceptable knowledge is the one which is being heard, not just received by way of *irsal*."[24]

9. Al-Khatib al-Baghdadi (d. 462) strongly supports the view of those who reject the Mursal except if it comes through an elder Successor. He concludes, after giving a perusal of different opinions about this issue,

> "What we select out of these sayings is that the *mursal* is not
> to be practised, nor is it acceptable as proof. We say that *irsal*
> leads to one reporter being ambiguous; if he is ambiguous, to
> ascertain his reliability is impossible. We have already
> explained that a narration is only acceptable if it comes
> through a reporter known for reliability. Hence, the *mursal*
> should not be accepted at all."[25]

Al-Khatib gives the following example, showing that a narrative which has been reported through both *musnad* and *mursal isnads* is acceptable, not because of the reliability of those who narrated it by way of *irsal* but because of an uninterrupted *isnad*, even though it contains less reliable reporters:

The text of the Hadith is: "No marriage is valid except by the consent of the guardian"; al- Khatib gives two *isnads* going back to Shu'bah and Sufyan al-Thauri; the remainder of each *isnad* is: Sufyan al-Thauri and Shu'bah --- Abu Ishaq --- Abu Burdah --- the Prophet ﷺ.

---

[23] Al-Hakim, p. 26.
[24] *Ibid.*
[25] Al-Khatib al-Baghdadi, *Al-Kifayah fi 'Ilm al- Riwayah* (Hyderabad, 1357), p. 387.

This *isnad* is *mursal* because Abu Burdah, a Successor, narrates directly from the Prophet ﷺ. However, al-Khatib further gives three *isnads* going back to Yunus b. Abi Ishaq, Isra'il b. Yunus and Qais b. al-Rabi'; the remainder of the first *isnad* is: Yunus b. Abi Ishaq --- Abu Ishaq --- Abu Burdah --- Abu Musa --- the Prophet ﷺ.

The other two reporters narrate similarly, both of them including the name of Abu Musa, the Companion from whom Abu Burdah has reported. Al-Khatib goes on to prove that both al-Thauri and Shu'bah heard this Hadith from Abu Ishaq in one sitting while the other three reporters heard it in different sittings. Hence, this addition of Abu Musa in the *isnad* is quite acceptable.[26]

10. **Ibn al-Salah (d. 643)** agrees with al-Shafi'i in rejecting the *mursal* Hadith unless it is proved to have come through a *musnad* route.[27]

11. **Ibn Taimiyyah (d. 728)** classifies *mursal* into three categories. He says,

> "There are some acceptable, others unacceptable, and some which require further investigation:
>
> - if it is known that the reporter does so (i.e. narrates by *irsal*) from reliable authorities, then his report will be accepted;
>
> - if he does so from both classes of authorities, i.e. reliable and unreliable, we shall not accept his narration (on its own, without further investigation), for he is narrating from someone whose reliability is unknown;

---

[26] Ibid, pp. 411-413.

[27] Zain al-Din al-'Iraqi, *Al-Taqyid wa 'l-Idah Sharh Muqaddimah Ibn al-Salah* (al-Maktabah al-Salafiyyahh, Madinah, 1389/1969), p. 72.

- all such *mursal Ahadith* which go against the reports made by reliable authorities will be rejected completely."[28]

12. Al-Dhahabi (d. 748) regards the *mursal* of younger Successors such as al-Hasan al-Basri, al- Zuhri, Qatadah and Humaid al-Tawil as the weakest type of *mursal.*[29]

Later scholars such as Ibn Kathir (d. 744), al-'Iraqi (d. 806), Ibn Hajar (d. 852), al-Suyuti (d. 911), Muhammad b. Ibrahim al-Wazir (d. 840), Jamal al-Din al-Qasimi (d. 1332) and Tahir al- Jaza'iri (d. 1338) have given exhaustive discussions about this issue, but none of them holds an opinion different to those mentioned above.

3) ACCORDING TO THE NUMBER OF REPORTERS INVOLVED IN EACH STAGE OF THE ISNAD

Mutawatir (متواتر) & *Ahad* (آحاد)

Depending on the number of the reporters of the Hadith in each stage of the *isnad*, i.e. in each generation of reporters, it can be classified into the general categories of *mutawatir* ("consecutive") or *ahad* ("single") Hadith.

A *mutawatir* Hadith is one which is reported by such a large number of people that they cannot be expected to agree upon a lie, all of them together.[30]

Al-Ghazali (d. 505) stipulates that a *mutawatir* narration be known by the sizeable number of its reporters equally in the beginning, in the middle and

---

[28] Ibn Taymiyyah, *Minhaj al-Sunnah an-Nabawiyyah fi Naqd Kalam al-Shi'ah wa 'l-Qadariyyah* (al- Maktabah al-Amiriyyah, Bulaq, 1322), 4:117.

[29] Al-Dhahabi, *Al-Muqizah* (Maktab al-Matbu'at al- Islamiyyah, Halab, 1405), p. 40.

[30] Al-Jaza'iri, p. 33.

at the end.[31] He is correct in this stipulation because some narrations or ideas, although known as *mutawatir* among some people, whether Muslims or non-Muslims, originally have no *tawatur*. There is no precise definition for a "large number of reporters"; although the numbers four, five, seven, ten, twelve, forty and seventy, among others, have all been variously suggested as a minimum, the exact number is irrelevant (some reporters, e.g. Imams of Hadith, carry more weight anyway than others who are their contemporaries): the important condition is that the possibility of coincidence or "organised falsehood" be obviously negligible.[32]

Examples of *mutawatir* practices are the five daily prayers, fasting, zakat, the Hajj and recitation of the Qur'an. Among the verbal *mutawatir Ahadith*, the following has been reported by at least sixty-two Companions from the Prophet ﷺ, and has been widely-known amongst the Muslims throughout the ages:

« من كذب علي متعمدا فليتبوأ مقعده من النار »

**"Whoever invents a lie and attributes it to me intentionally,
let him prepare his seat in the Fire."**

Ahadith related to the description of the *Haud Kauthar* (the Basin of Abundant Goodness) in the Hereafter, raising the hands at certain postures during prayer, rubbing wet hands on the leather socks during ablution, revelation of the Qur'an in seven modes, and the prohibition of every intoxicant are further examples of verbal *mutawatir Ahadith*.[33]

A Hadith *ahad* or *khabar wahid* is one which is narrated by people whose number does not reach that of the *mutawatir* case. *Ahad* is further classified into:

---

[31] *Ibid.*

[32] Ibn Hajar al-'Asqalani, *Sharh Nukhbah al-Fikr* (ed. M. 'Aud & M.G. Sabbagh, Damascus, 1410/1990), pp. 8-9.

[33] Al-Jaza'iri, p. 49; Muhammad b. Isma'il al- Amir al-San'ani, *Taudih al-Afkar* (2 vols. ed. M.M. 'Abdul Hamid, Cairo, 1366), 2:405.

Gharib (غريب), *'Aziz* (عزيز) & *Mashhur* (مشهور)

A Hadith is termed *gharib* ("scarce, strange") when only a single reporter is found relating it at some stage of the *isnad*. For example, the saying of the Prophet ﷺ,

« السفر قطعة من العذاب »

"Travel is a piece of punishment" is *gharib*; the *isnad* of this Hadith contains only one reporter in each stage: Malik --- Yahya b. Abi Salih --- Abu Hurairah --- the Prophet ﷺ. With regard to its *isnad*, this Hadith is *sahih*, although most *gharib Ahadith* are weak; Ahmad b. Hanbal said, "Do not write these *gharib Ahadith* because they are unacceptable, and most of them are weak."[34]

A type of Hadith similar to *gharib* is *fard* ("solitary"); it is known in three ways:

i. Similar to gharib, i.e. a single person is found reporting it from a well-known Imam;
ii. The people of one locality only are known to narrate the Hadith;
iii. Narrators from one locality report the Hadith from narrators of another locality, such as the people of Makkah reporting from the people of Madinah.[35]

If at any stage in the *isnad*, only two reporters are found to narrate the Hadith, it is termed *'aziz* ("rare, strong"). For example, Anas reported that the Messenger of Allah ﷺ said,

« لا يؤمن أحدكم حتى أكون أحب إليه من والده وولده والناس أجمعين »

**"None of you (truly) believes until I become more beloved to
him than his father, his son, and all the people."**

---

[34] Al-San'ani, 2:409.
[35] Al-Hakim, pp. 96-102.

Two reporters, Qatadah and 'Abdul 'Aziz b. Shu'aib, report this Hadith from Anas, and two more reporters narrate from each of them: Shu'bah and Sa'id report from Qatada, and Isma'il b. Ulayyah and 'Abd al-Warith from 'Abd al-'Aziz; then a group of people report from each of them.[36]

A Hadith which is reported by more than two reporters is known as *mashhur* ("famous"). According to some scholars, every narrative which comes to be known widely, whether or not it has an authentic origin, is called *mashhur*. A *mashhur* Hadith might be reported by only one or two reporters in the beginning but become widely-known later, unlike *gharib* or *'aziz*, which are reported by one or two reporters in the beginning and continue to have the same number even in the times of the Successors and those after them. For example, if only one or two reporters are found narrating Hadith from a reliable authority in Hadith such as al-Zuhri and Qatadah, the Hadith will remain either *gharib* or *'aziz*. On the other hand, if a group of people narrate from them, it will be known as *mashhur*.[37]

According to al-'Ala'i (Abu Sa'id Khalil Salah al-Din, d. 761), a Hadith may be known as *'aziz* and *mashhur* at the same time. By this he means a Hadith which is left with only two reporters in its *isnad* at any stage while it enjoys a host of reporters in other stages, such as the saying of the Prophet ﷺ,

» نحن الآخرون السابقون يوم القيامة «

"We are the last but (will be) the foremost on the Day of Resurrection."

This Hadith is *'aziz* in its first stage, as it is reported by Hudhaifah b. al-Yaman and Abu Hurairah only. It later becomes *mashhur* as seven people report it from Abu Hurairah.[38]

---

[36] Al-San'ani, 2:455.
[37] Al-'Iraqi, p. 268.
[38] Al-San'ani, 2:406.

4) ACCORDING TO THE MANNER IN WHICH THE HADITH IS REPORTED

Mudallas (مدلس) Hadith & *Tadlis*

Different ways of reporting, e.g. حدثنا (he narrated to us), أخبرنا (he informed us), سمعت (I heard), and عن (on the authority of) are used by the reporters of Hadith. The first three indicate that the reporter personally heard from his *shaykh*, whereas the fourth mode can denote either hearing in person or through another reporter.

A *mudallas* ("concealed") Hadith is one which is weak due to the uncertainty caused by *tadlis*. *Tadlis* (concealing) refers to an *isnad* where a reporter has concealed the identity of his *shaykh*. Ibn al-Salah describes two types of *tadlis*:

i. *Tadlis al-isnad.* A person reports from his *shaykh* whom he met, what he did not hear from him, or from a contemporary of his whom he did not meet, in such a way as to create the impression that he heard the Hadith in person. A *mudallis* (one who practises *tadlis*) here usually uses the mode عن ("on the authority of") or قال ("he said") to conceal the truth about the *isnad*.

ii. *Tadlis al-shuyukh.* The reporter does mention his *shaykh* by name, but uses a less well-known name, by-name, nickname etc., in order not to disclose his *shaykh's* identity.[39]

Al-'Iraqi (d. 806), in his notes on *Muqaddimah Ibn al-Salah*, adds a third type of *tadlis*:

iii. *Tadlis al-taswiyyah.* To explain it, let us assume an *isnad* which contains a trustworthy *shaykh* reporting from a weak authority, who in turn reports from another trustworthy *shaykh*. Now, the

---

[39] Al-'Iraqi, p. 96.

reporter of this *isnad* omits the intermediate weak authority, leaving it apparently consisting of reliable authorities. He plainly shows that he heard it from his *shaykh* but he uses the mode "on the authority of" to link his immediate *shaykh* with the next trustworthy one. To an average student, this *isnad* seems free of any doubt or discrepancy. This is known to have been practised by Baqiyyah b. al-Walid, Walid b. Muslim, al-A'mash and al-Thauri. It is said to be the worst among the three kinds of *tadlis*.[40]

Ibn Hajar classifies those who practised *tadlis* into five categories in his essay *Tabaqat al-Mudallisin*:

- Those who are known to do it occasionally, such as Yahya b. Sa'id al-Ansari.

- Those who are accepted by the traditionists, either because of their good reputation and relatively few cases of *tadlis*, e.g. Sufyan al-Thauri (d. 161), or because they reported from authentic authorities only, e.g. Sufyan Ibn 'Uyainah (d. 198).

- Those who practised it a great deal, and the traditionists have accepted such *Ahadith* from them which were reported with a clear mention of hearing directly. Among these are Abu 'l- Zubair al-Makki, whose *Ahadith* narrated from the Companion Jabir b. 'Abdullah have been collected in *Sahih Muslim*. Opinions differ regarding whether they are acceptable or not.

- Similar to the previous category, but the traditionists agree that their *Ahadith* are to be rejected unless they clearly admit of their hearing, such as by saying "I heard"; an example of this category is Baqiyyah b. al-Walid.

- Those who are disparaged due to another reason apart from *tadlis*; their *Ahadith* are rejected, even though they admit of hearing them directly. Exempted from them are reporters such as Ibn Lahi'ah,

---

[40] *Ibid.*

the famous Egyptian judge, whose weakness is found to be of a lesser degree. Ibn Hajar gives the names of 152 such reporters.[41]

Tadlis, especially of those in the last three categories, is so disliked that Shu'bah (d. 170) said, "*Tadlis* is the brother of lying" and "To commit adultery is more favourable to me than to report by way of *Tadlis*."[42]

Musalsal (مسلسل)

A *musalsal* (uniformly-linked) *isnad* is one in which all the reporters, as well as the Prophet ﷺ, use the same mode of transmission such as 'an, *haddathana*, etc., repeat any other additional statement or remark, or act in a particular manner while narrating the Hadith.

Al-Hakim gives eight examples of such *isnads*, each having a different characteristic repeated feature:

- use of the phrase *sami'tu* (I heard);
- the expression "stand and pour water for me so that I may illustrate the way my *shaykh* performed ablution";
- *haddathana* (he narrated to us);
- *amarani* (he commanded me);
- holding one's beard;
- illustrating by counting on five fingers;
- the expression "I testify that ..."; and
- interlocking the fingers.[43]

Knowledge of *musalsal* helps in discounting the possibility of *tadlis*.

---

[41] Ibn Hajar, *Tabaqat al-Mudallisin* (Cairo, 1322), p. 7f.
[42] Al-'Iraqi, p. 98.
[43] Al-Hakim, pp. 30-34.

5) ACCORDING TO THE NATURE OF THE TEXT AND *ISNAD*

Shadhdh (شاذ) & *Munkar* (منكر)

According to al-Shafi'i, a *shadhdh* ("irregular") Hadith is one which is reported by a trustworthy person but goes against the narration of a person more reliable than him. It does not include a Hadith which is unique in its contents and is not narrated by someone else.[44] In the light of this definition, the well-known Hadith,

» إنما الأعمال بالنيات «

"Actions are (judged) according to their intentions", is not considered *shadhdh* since it has been narrated by Yahya b. Sa'id al-Ansari from Muhammad b. Ibrahim al-Taimi from 'Alqamah from 'Umar, all of whom are trustworthy authorities, although each one of them is the only reporter at that stage.[45]

An example of a *shadhdh* Hadith according to some scholars is one which Abu Dawud and al-Tirmidhi transmit, through the following *isnad*: 'Abdul Wahid b. Ziyad --- al-A'mash --- Abu Salih --- Abu Hurairah === the Prophet ﷺ: "When one of you offers the two rak'ahs before the Dawn Prayer, he should lie down on his right side."

Regarding it, al-Baihaqi said,

> "'Abdul Wahid has gone against a large number of people with this narration, for they have reported the above as an act of the Prophet ﷺ, and not as his saying; 'Abdul Wahid is alone

---

[44] *Ibid*, p. 119.

[45] Ibn Kathir, *Ikhtisar 'Ulum al-Hadith* (ed. Ahmad Shakir, 2nd imp., Cairo, 1951), p. 57.

amongst the trustworthy students of al-A'mash in narrating these words."[46]

According to Ibn Hajar, if a narration which goes against another authentic Hadith is reported by a weak narrator, it is known as *munkar* (denounced).[47] Traditionists as late as Ahmad used to simply label any Hadith of a weak reporter as *munkar*.[48] Sometimes, a Hadith is labelled as *munkar* because of its contents being contrary to general sayings of the Prophet ﷺ. Al-Khatib (d. 463) quotes al-Rabi' b. Khaitham (d. 63) as saying, "Some *Ahadith* have a light like that of day, which we recognise; others have a darkness like that of night which makes us reject them."

He also quotes al-Auza'i (d. 157) as saying,

> "We used to listen to *Ahadith* and present them to fellow traditionists, just as we present forged coins to money-changers: whatever they recognise of them, we accept, and whatever they reject of them, we also reject."[49]

Ibn Kathir quotes the following two *Ahadith* in his *Tafsir*, the first of which is acceptable, whereas the second contradicts it and is unreliable:

i.   Ahmad === Abu Mu'awiyah === Hisham b. 'Urwah --- Fatimah bint al-Mundhir --- Asma' bint Abi Bakr, who said, "My mother came (to Madinah) during the treaty Quraish had made, while she was still a polytheist. So I came to the Prophet ﷺ and said to him, 'O Messenger of Allah, my mother has come willingly: should I treat her with kindness?' He replied, 'Yes! Treat her with kindness'."

ii. Al-Bazzar === 'Abdullah b. Shabib === Abu Bakr b. Abi Shaibah === Abu Qatadah al-'Adawi -- the nephew of al-Zuhri --- al-Zuhri ---

---

[46] Al-Suyuti, 1:235; M. A. Salih, p. 260.
[47] Al-San'ani, 2:3.
[48] *Ibid*, 2:6.
[49] Al-Khatib, p. 431.

> 'Urwah --- 'A'ishah and Asma', both of whom said, "Our mother came to us in Madinah while she was a polytheist, during the peace treaty between the Quraish and the Messenger of Allah ﷺ. So we said, 'O Messenger of Allah, our mother has come to Madinah willingly: do we treat her kindly?' He said, 'Yes! Treat her kindly'."

Ibn Kathir then remarks: "This (latter) Hadith, to our knowledge is reported only through this route of al- Zuhri --- 'Urwah --- 'A'ishah. It is a *munkar* Hadith with this text because the mother of 'A'ishah is Umm Ruman, who was already a Muslim emigrant, while the mother of Asma' was another woman, as mentioned by name in other *Ahadith*."[50]

In contrast to a *munkar* Hadith, if a reliable reporter is found to add something which is not narrated by other authentic sources, the addition is accepted as long as it does not contradict them; and is known as *ziyadatu thiqah* (an addition by one trustworthy).[51] An example is the Hadith of al-Bukhari and Muslim on the authority of Ibn Mas'ud: "I asked the Messenger of Allah ﷺ, 'Which action is the most virtuous?' He said, 'The Prayer at its due time'." Two reporters, Al-Hasan b. Makdam and Bundar, reported it with the addition, "... at the beginning of its time"; both Al-Hakim and Ibn Hibban declared this addition to be *sahih*.[52]

Mudraj (مدرج)

An addition by a reporter to the text of the saying being narrated is termed *mudraj* (interpolated).[53] For example, al-Khatib relates via Abu Qattan and Shababah --- Shu'bah --- Muhammad b. Ziyad --- Abu Hurairah --- The Prophet ﷺ, who said,

---

[50] Ibn Kathir, *Tafsir*, 4:349.
[51] Ibn Kathir, *Ikhtisar*, p. 62.
[52] Al-Suyuti, 1:248.
[53] Al-Hakim, p. 39.

» إسبغوا الوضوع، ويل للأعقاب من النار «

"Perform the ablution fully; woe to the heels from the Fire!"

Al-Khatib then remarks,

> "The statement, 'Perform the ablution fully' is made by Abu Hurairah, while the statement afterwards, 'Woe to the heels from the Fire!' is that of the Prophet ﷺ. The distinction between the two is understood from the narration of al-Bukhari, who transmits the same Hadith and quotes Abu Hurairah as saying, 'Complete the ablution, for Abu 'l-Qasim ﷺ said: Woe to the heels from the Fire!'"[54]

Such an addition may be found in the beginning, in the middle, or at the end, often in explanation of a term used. *Idraj* (interpolation) is mostly found in the text, although a few examples show that such additions are found in the *isnad* as well, where the reporter grafts a part of one *isnad* into another.

A reporter found to be in the habit of intentional *idraj* is generally unacceptable and considered a liar.[55] However, the traditionists are more lenient towards those reporters who may do so forgetfully or in order to explain a difficult word.

6) ACCORDING TO A HIDDEN DEFECT FOUND IN THE *ISNAD* OR TEXT OF A HADITH

Before discussing *ma'lul* (defective) *Ahadith*, a brief note on *mudtarib* (shaky) and *maqlub* (reversed) *Ahadith* would help in understanding *ma'lul*.

---

[54] Al-'Iraqi, p. 129f.
[55] Al-Suyuti, 1:274.

Mudtarib (مضطرب)

According to Ibn Kathir, if reporters disagree about a particular *shaykh*, or about some other points in the *isnad* or the text, in such a way that none of the opinions can be preferred over the others, and thus there is uncertainty about the *isnad* or text, such a Hadith is called *mudtarib* (shaky).[56]

For example with regard to *idtirab* in the *isnad*, it is reported on the authority of Abu Bakr that he said, "O Messenger of Allah! I see you getting older?" He ﷺ replied, "What made me old are *Surah Hud* and its sister *surahs*." Al-Daraqutni says,

> "This is an example of a *mudtarib* Hadith. It is reported through Abu Ishaq, but as many as ten different opinions are held about this *isnad*: some report it as *mursal*, others as *muttasil*; some take it as *musnad* of Abu Bakr, others as *musnad* of Sa'd or 'A'ishah. Since all these reports are comparable in weight, it is difficult to prefer one above another. Hence, the Hadith is termed as *mudtarib*."[57]

As an example of *idtirab* in the text, Rafi' b. Khadij said that the Messenger of Allah ﷺ forbade the renting of land. The reporters narrating from Rafi' give different statements, as follows:

i. Hanzalah asked Rafi', "What about renting for gold and silver?" He replied, "It does not matter if it is rent for gold and silver."

ii. Rifa'ah --- Rafi' --- the Prophet ﷺ, who said, "Whoever owns a piece of land should cultivate it, give it to his brother to cultivate, or abandon it."

iii. Salim --- Rafi' --- his two uncles --- the Prophet ﷺ, who forbade the renting of farming land.

---

[56] Ibn Kathir, *Ikhtisar*, p. 72.
[57] *Ibid.*

iv. The son of Rafi' --- Rafi' --- the Prophet ﷺ, who forbade the renting of land.

v. A different narration by Rafi' from the Prophet ﷺ, who said, "Whoever owns a piece of land should either cultivate it or give it to his brother to cultivate. He must not rent it for a third or a quarter of the produce, nor for a given quantity of the produce."

vi. Zaid b. Thabit said, "May Allah forgive Rafi'! I am more aware of the Hadith than he; what happened was that two of the Ansar (Helpers) had a dispute, so they came to the Prophet ﷺ, who said after listening to their cases, 'If this is your position, then do not rent the farms.' Rafi' has only heard the last phrase, i.e., 'Do not rent the farms'."

Because of these various versions, Ahmad b. Hanbal said, "The *Ahadith* reported by Rafi' about the renting of land are *mudtarib*. They are not to be accepted, especially when they go against the well-established Hadith of Ibn 'Umar that the Messenger of Allah ﷺ gave the land of Khaibar to the Jews on condition that they work on it and take half of the produce."[58]

Maqlub (مقلوب)

A Hadith is known as *maqlub* (changed, reversed) when its *isnad* is grafted to a different text or vice versa, or if a reporter happens to reverse the order of a sentence in the text.

As an example relating to the text, in his transmission of the famous Hadith describing the seven who will be under the shelter of Allah on the Day of Judgment, Muslim reports one of the categories as, "a man who conceals his act of charity to such an extent that his right hand does not know what his left hand gives in charity." This sentence has clearly been reversed by a

---

[58] Ibn 'Abdul Barr, *Al-Tamhid*, 3:32, as quoted by Luqman al-Salafi, *Ihtimam al-Muhaddithin bi Naqd al-Hadith*, p. 381f.

reporter, because the correct wording is recorded in other narrations of both al-Bukhari and Muslim as follows: "**... that his left hand does not know what his right hand gives ...**"[59]

The famous trial of al-Bukhari by the scholars of Baghdad provides a good example of a *maqlub isnad*. The traditionists, in order to test their visitor, al-Bukhari, appointed ten men, each with ten *Ahadith*. Now, each Hadith (text) of these ten people was prefixed with the *isnad* of another. Imam al-Bukhari listened to each of the ten men as they narrated their *Ahadith* and denied the correctness of every Hadith. When they had finished narrating these *Ahadith*, he addressed each person in turn and recounted to him each of his *Ahadith* with its correct *isnad*. This trial earned him great honour among the scholars of Baghdad.[60]

Other ways in which *Ahadith* have been rendered *maqlub* are by replacement of the name of a reporter with another, e.g. quoting Abu Hurairah as the reporter from the Prophet ﷺ although the actual reporter was someone else, or by reversal of the name of the reporter, e.g. mentioning Walid b. Muslim instead of Muslim b. Walid, or Ka'b b. Murrah instead of Murrah b. Ka'b.[61]

Ma'lul or *Mu'allal* (معلل، معلول)

Ibn al-Salah says, "A *ma'lul* (defective) Hadith is one which appears to be sound, but thorough research reveals a disparaging factor." Such factors can be:

i.   Declaring a Hadith *musnad* when it is in fact *mursal*, or *marfu'* when it is in fact *mauquf*;

---

[59] Ibn Kathir, *Ikhtisar*, p. 88.
[60] *Ibid*, p. 87.
[61] Shams al-Din Muhammad b. 'Abd al-Rahman al- Sakhawi, *Fath al-Mughith Sharh Alfiyyah al-Hadith li 'l-'Iraqi* (Lucknow, N.D.), 1:278.

ii.   Showing a reporter to narrate from his *shaykh* when in fact he did
        not meet the latter; or attributing a Hadith to one Companion
        when it in fact comes through another.[62]

Ibn al-Madini (d. 324) says that such a defect can only be revealed if all the
isnads of a particular Hadith are collated. In his book *al-'Ilal*, he gives thirty-
four Successors and the names of those Companions from whom each of
them heard *Ahadith* directly. For example, he says that al-Hasan al-Basri (d.
110, aged 88) did not see 'Ali (d. 40), although he adds that there is a slight
possibility that he may have seen him during his childhood in Madinah.[63]
Such information is very important, since for example, many Sufi traditions
go back to al- Hasan al-Basri, who is claimed to report directly from 'Ali.

Being a very delicate branch of *Mustalah al-Hadith*, only a few well-known
traditionists such as Ibn al-Madini (d. 234), Ibn Abi Hatim al-Razi (d. 327),
al-Khallal (d. 311) and al-Daraqutni (d. 385), have compiled books about it.
Ibn Abi Hatim, in his *Kitab al-'Ilal*, has given 2840 examples of *ma'lul*
Ahadith about a range of topics.

An example of a *ma'lul* Hadith is one transmitted by Muslim on the
authority of Abu Hurairah, who reports the Prophet ﷺ as saying,

> "Allah created the land on Saturday; He created the
> mountains on Sunday; He created the trees on Monday; He
> created the things entailing labour on Tuesday; He created
> the light (or fish) on Wednesday; He scattered the beasts in
> it (the earth) on Thursday; and He created Adam after the

---

[62] 'Uthman b. 'Abd al-Rahman al-Dimashqi Ibn al- Salah, *'Ulum al-Hadith* (commonly known
as *Muqaddimah*, ed. al-Tabbakh, Halab, 1350), p. 116.

[63] 'Ali b. 'Abdullah b. Ja'far Ibn al-Madini, *Kitab al-'Ilal*, p. 58. Ibn Hajar al-'Asqalani mentions
that the Imams of Hadith have agreed that al-Hasan al-Basri did not hear a single word from
'Ali.

afternoon of Friday, the last creation at the last hour of the hours of Friday, between the afternoon and night."[64]

Regarding it, Ibn Taimiyyah says,

> "Men more knowledgeable than Muslim, such as al-Bukhari and Yahya b. Ma'in, have criticised it. Al-Bukhari said, 'This saying is not that of the Prophet ﷺ, but one of Ka'b al-Ahbar'."[65]

7) ACCORDING TO THE RELIABILITY AND MEMORY OF THE REPORTERS

The final verdict on a Hadith, i.e. *sahih* (sound), *hasan* (good), *da'if* (weak) or *maudu'* (fabricated, forged), depends critically on this factor.

Among the early traditionists, mostly of the first two centuries, *Ahadith* were classified into two categories only: *sahih* and *da'if*; al-Tirmidhi was to be the first to distinguish *hasan* from *da'if*. This is why traditionists and jurists such as Ahmad, who seemed to argue on the basis of *da'if Ahadith*

---

[64] *Sahih* Muslim, 4:2149 (English transl., IV:1462, *Sharh Nawawi*, 17:133).

[65] Ibn Taimiyyah, *Majmu' Fatawa* (37 vols., ed. 'Abd al-Rahman b. Qasim & his son Muhammad, Riyad, 1398), 18:18f. Ibn Taimiyyah mentions that Imam Muslim's authentication of this hadith is supported by Abu Bakr al-Anbari & Ibn al- Jauzi, whereas al-Baihaqi supports those who disparaged it. Al-Albani says that it was Ibn al-Madini who criticised it, whereas Ibn Ma'in did not (the latter was known to be very strict, both of them were shaikhs of al-Bukhari). He further says that the hadith is sahih, and does not contradict the Qur'an, contrary to the probable view of the scholars who criticised the hadith, since what is mentioned in the Qur'an is the creation of the heavens and the earth in six days, each of which may be like a thousand years, whereas the hadith refers to the creation of the earth only, in days which are shorter than those referred to in the Qur'an (*Silsilah al-Ahadith as-Sahihah*, no. 1833).

sometimes, were in fact basing their argument on the *Ahadith* which were later to be known as *hasan*.[66]

We now examine in more detail these four important classes of *Ahadith*.

Sahih (صحيح)

Al-Shafi'i states the following requirement in order for a Hadith which is not *mutawatir* to be acceptable:

> "Each reporter should be trustworthy in his religion; he should be known to be truthful in his narrating, to understand what he narrates, to know how a different expression can alter the meaning, and report the wording of the Hadith verbatim, not only its meaning. This is because if he does not know how a different expression can change the whole meaning, he will not know if he has changed what is lawful into what is prohibited. Hence, if he reports the Hadith according to its wording, no change of meaning will be found at all. Moreover, he should be a good memoriser if he happens to report from his memory, or a good preserver of his writings if he happens to report from them. He should agree with the narrations of the *huffaz* (leading authorities in Hadith), if he reports something which they do also. He should not be a *mudallis*, who narrates from someone he met something he did not hear, nor should he report from the Prophet ﷺ contrary to what reliable sources have reported from him. In addition, the one who is above him (in the *isnad*) should be of the same

---

[66] Al-Dhahabi, p. 27.

quality, [and so on,] until the Hadith goes back uninterrupted to the Prophet ﷺ or any authority below him."[67]

Ibn al-Salah, however, defines a *sahih* Hadith more precisely by saying:

"A *sahih* Hadith is the one which has a continuous *isnad*, made up of reporters of trustworthy memory from similar authorities, and which is found to be free from any irregularities (i.e. in the text) or defects (i.e. in the *isnad*)."

By the above definition, no room is left for any weak Hadith, whether, for example, it is *munqati', mu'dal, mudtarib, maqlub, shadhdh, munkar, ma'lul,* or contains a *mudallis*. The definition also excludes *hasan Ahadith*, as will be discussed under that heading.

Of all the collectors of Hadith, al-Bukhari and Muslim were greatly admired because of their tireless attempts to collect *sahih Ahadith* only. It is generally understood that the more trustworthy and of good memory the reporters, the more authentic the Hadith. The *isnad*: al- Shafi'i --- Malik --- Nafi' --- 'Abdullah b. 'Umar --- The Prophet ﷺ, is called a "golden *isnad*" because of its renowned reporters.[68]

Some traditionists prefer *Sahih al-Bukhari* to *Sahih Muslim* because al-Bukhari always looked for those reporters who had either accompanied or met each other, even if only once in their lifetime. On the other hand, Muslim would accept a reporter who is simply found to be contemporary to his immediate authority in reporting.[69]

The following grading is given for *sahih Ahadith* only:

1. those which are transmitted by both al- Bukhari and Muslim;
2. those which are transmitted by al-Bukhari only;

---

[67] Al-Shafi'i, p. 37of (Eng. trans., pp. 239- 240).
[68] Al-Dhahabi, p. 24.
[69] Al-Nawawi, *Muqaddimah*, p. 14.

3. those which are transmitted by Muslim only;

   Those which are not found in the above two collections, but

4. which agree with the requirements of both al-Bukhari and Muslim;

5. which agree with the requirements of al-Bukhari only;

6. which agree with the requirements of Muslim only; and

7. those declared *sahih* by other traditionists.[70]

Hasan (حسن)

Al-Tirmidhi means by Hadith *hasan*: a Hadith which is not *shadhdh*, nor contains a disparaged reporter in its *isnad*, and which is reported through more than one route of narration.[71]

Al-Khattabi (d. 388) states a very concise definition, "It is the one where its source is known and its reporters are unambiguous."

By this he means that the reporters of the Hadith should not be of a doubtful nature, such as with the *mursal* or *munqati'* Hadith, or one containing a *mudallis*.

Ibn al-Salah classifies *hasan* into two categories:

i. one with an *isnad* containing a reporter who is *mastur* ("screened", i.e. no prominent person reported from him) but is not totally careless in his reporting, provided that a similar text is reported through another *isnad* as well;

ii. one with an *isnad* containing a reporter who is known to be truthful and reliable, but is a degree less in his preservation/memory of Hadith in comparison to the reporters of *sahih Ahadith*.

---

[70] Al-Tibi, al-Husain b. 'Abdullah, *al-Khulasah fi Usul al-Hadith* (ed. Subhi al-Samarra'i, Baghdad, 1391), p. 36.

[71] *Ibid*, p. 38.

In both categories, Ibn al-Salah requires that the Hadith be free of any *shudhudh* (irregularities).[72]

Al-Dhahabi, after giving the various definitions, says, "A *hasan* Hadith is one which excels the *da'if* but nevertheless does not reach the standard of a sahih Hadith."[73]

In the light of this definition, the following *isnads* are *hasan* according to al-Dhahabi:

   i.   Bahz b. Ḥakam --- his father --- his grandfather;

   ii.   'Amr b. Shu'aib --- his father --- his grandfather;

   iii.   Muhammad b. 'Amr --- Abu Salamah --- Abu Hurairah.

Reporters such as al-Harith b. 'Abdullah, 'Asim b. Damurah, Hajjaj b. Artat, Khusaif b. 'Abd al- Rahman and Darraj Abu al-Samh attract different verdicts: some traditionists declare their *Ahadith hasan*, others declare them *da'if*.[74]

Example of a *hasan* Hadith: Malik, Abu Dawud, al-Tirmidhi and al-Hakim reported through their *isnads* from 'Amr b. Shu'aib --- his father --- his grandfather, that the Messenger of Allah ﷺ said,

» الراكب شيطان، والراكبان شيطانان والثلاثة ركب «

"A single rider is a devil (i.e. disobedient), two riders are two devils, but three makes a travelling party."

---

[72] Al-Nawawi, *Muqaddimah*, p. 43.
[73] Al-Dhahabi, p. 26.
[74] *Ibid*, pp. 32-33.

Al-Tirmidhi declares this Hadith to be *hasan* because of the above *isnad*, which falls short of the requirements for a *sahih* Hadith.[75]

Several weak *Ahadith* may mutually support each other to the level of *hasan*.

According to the definitions of al-Tirmidhi and Ibn al-Salah, a number of similar weak *Ahadith* on a particular issue can be raised to the degree of *hasan* if the weakness found in their reporters is of a mild nature. Such a Hadith is known as *hasan li ghairihi* (*hasan* due to others), to distinguish it from the type previously-discussed, which is *hasan li dhatihi* (*hasan* in itself). Similarly, several *hasan Ahadith* on the same subject may make the Hadith *sahih li ghairihi*, to be distinguished from the previously-discussed *sahih li dhatihi*.

However, in case the weakness is severe (e.g., the reporter is accused of lying or the Hadith is itself *shadhdh*), such very weak *Ahadith* will not support each other and will remain weak. For example, the well-known Hadith,

» مـن حفـظ علـى أمتـي أربعـين حـديثا بعثـه الله يـوم القيامـة فـي زمـرة الفقهاء «

"He who preserves forty *Ahadith* for my *Ummah* will be raised by Allah on the Day of Resurrection among the men of understanding", has been declared to be *da'if* by most of the traditionists, although it is reported through several routes.[76]

---

[75] Al-Albani, *Silsilah al-Ahadith al-Sahihah*, no. 62.
[76] Al-Jaza'iri, p. 149.

Da'if (ضعيف)

A Hadith which fails to reach the status of *hasan* is *da'if*. Usually, the weakness is one of discontinuity in the *isnad*, in which case the Hadith could be *mursal, mu'allaq, mudallas, munqati'* or *mu'dal*, according to the precise nature of the discontinuity, or one of a reporter having a disparaged character, such as due to his telling lies, excessive mistakes, opposition to the narration of more reliable sources, involvement in innovation, or ambiguity surrounding his person.

The smaller the number and importance of defects, the less severe the weakness. The more the defects in number and severity, the closer the Hadith will be to being *maudu'* (fabricated).[77]

Some *Ahadith*, according to the variation in the nature of the weakness associated with its reporters, rank at the bottom of the *hasan* grade or at the top of the *da'if* grade. Reporters such as 'Abdullah b. Lahi'ah (a famous judge from Egypt), 'Abd al-Rahman b. Zaid b. Aslam, Abu Bakr b. Abi Maryam al-Himsi, Faraj b. Fadalah, and Rishdin b. Sa'd attract such types of varying ranks as they are neither extremely good preservers nor totally abandoned by the traditionists.[78]

Maudu' (موضوع)

Al-Dhahabi defines *maudu'* (fabricated, forged) as the term applied to a Hadith, the text of which goes against the established norms of the Prophet's sayings ﷺ, or its reporters include a liar, e.g. the *Forty Ahadith* known as *Wad'aniyyah* or the small collection of *Ahadith* which was

---

[77] Al-Sakhawi, 1:99.
[78] Al-Dhahabi, pp. 33-34.

fabricated and claimed to have been reported by 'Ali al-Rida, the eighth Imam of the Ithna 'Ashari Shi'ah.[79]

A number of traditionists have collected fabricated *Ahadith* separately in order to distinguish them from other *Ahadith*; among them are Ibn al-Jauzi in *al-Maudu'at*, al-Jauzaqani in *Kitab al-Abatil*, al-Suyuti in *al-La'ali al-Masnu'ah fi 'l-Ahadith al-Maudu'ah*, and 'Ali al-Qari in *al-Maudu'at*.

Some of these *Ahadith* were known to be spurious by the confession of their inventors. For example, Muhammad b. Sa'id al-Maslub used to say, "It is not wrong to fabricate an *isnad* for a sound statement."[80] Another notorious inventor, 'Abd al-Karim Abu 'l-Auja, who was killed and crucified by Muhammad b. Sulaiman b. 'Ali, governor of Basrah, admitted that he had fabricated four thousand *Ahadith* declaring lawful the prohibited and vice-versa.[81]

Maudu' Ahadith are also recognised by external evidence related to a discrepancy found in the dates or times of a particular incident.[82] For example, when the second caliph, 'Umar b. al- Khattab decided to expel the Jews from Khaibar, some Jewish dignitaries brought a document to 'Umar apparently proving that the Prophet ﷺ had intended that they stay there by exempting them from the *jizyah* (tax on non-Muslims under the rule of Muslims); the document carried the witness of two Companions, Sa'd b. Mu'adh and Mu'awiyah b. Abi Sufyan. 'Umar rejected the document outright, knowing that it was fabricated because the conquest of Khaibar took place in 6 AH, whereas Sa'd b. Mu'adh died in 3 AH just after the Battle

---

[79] *Ibid*, p. 36.
[80] Al-Sakhawi, 1:264.
[81] *Ibid*, 1:275.
[82] Al-Nawawi, *Taqrib*, 1:275.

of the Trench, and Mu'awiyah embraced Islam in 8 AH, after the conquest of Makkah![83]

The author, in his *Criticism of Hadith Among Muslims with Reference to Sunan Ibn Majah*, has given more examples of fabricated *Ahadith* under the following eight categories of causes of fabrication:[84]

1. political differences;
2. factions based on issues of creed;
3. fabrications by *zanadiqah* (enemies-within spreading heretical beliefs);
4. fabrications by story-tellers;
5. fabrications by ignorant ascetics;
6. prejudice in favour of town, race or a particular imam;
7. inventions for personal motives;
8. proverbs turned into *Ahadith*.

Similar to the last category above is the case of *Isra'iliyat* ("Israelite traditions"), narrations from the Jews and the Christians[85] which were wrongly attributed to the Prophet ﷺ.

---

[83] See Ibn al-Qayyim, *al-Manar al-Munif fi 'l- Sahih wa 'l-Da'if* (ed. A.F. Abu Ghuddah, Lahore, 1402/1982), pp. 102-105 for a fuller discussion. Ibn al-Qayyim mentions more than ten clear indications of the forgery of the document, which the Jews repeatedly attempted to use to deceive the Muslims over the centuries, but each time a scholar of Hadith intervened to point out the forgery - such incidents occurred with Ibn Jarir al-Tabari (d. 310), al-Khatib al-Baghdadi (d. 463) and Ibn Taimiyyah (d. 728), who spat on the document as it was unfolded from beneath its silken covers.

[84] Suhaib Hasan, *Criticism of Hadith*, pp. 35-44.

[85] The Prophet ﷺ allowed such narrations, but they are not to be confirmed nor denied, except for what is confirmed or denied by the Qur'an and Sunnah. See e.g. *An Introduction to the Principles of Tafseer* of Ibn Taimiyyah (trans. M.A.H. Ansari, Al-Hidaayah, Birmingham, 1414/1993), pp. 56-58.

SECTION C:
FURTHER BRANCHES OF *MUSTALAH*
AND *RIJAL AL-HADITH*

The above-mentioned classification of *Ahadith* plays a vital role in ascertaining the authenticity of a particular narration. Ibn al-Salah mentions sixty-five terms in his book, of which twenty-three have been discussed above. Two further types not included by Ibn al-Salah, *mu'allaq* and *mutawatir*, have been dealt with from other sources. The remaining forty-two types follow in brief, which help further distinguish between different types of narrations.

1. Knowledge of *i'tibar* ("consideration"), *mutaba'ah* ("follow-up") and *shawahid* ("witnesses").

Traditionists are always in search of strengthening support for a Hadith which is reported by one source only; such research is termed *i'tibar*. If a supporting narration is not found for a particular Hadith, it is declared as *fard mutlaq* (absolutely singular) or *gharib*. For example, if a Hadith is reported through the following *isnad*: Hammad b. Salamah - -- Ayyub --- Ibn Sirin --- Abu Hurairah --- the Prophet ﷺ, research would be done to ascertain whether another trustworthy reporter has narrated it from Ayyub; if so, it will be called *mutaba'ah tammah* (full follow-up); if not, a reporter other than Ayyub narrating from Ibn Sirin would be sought: if so, it will be called *mutaba'ah qasirah* (incomplete follow-up). Whereas *mutaba'ah* applies to the *isnad*, i.e. other narrations from the same reporters, a narration which supports the text (meaning) of the original Hadith, although it may be through a completely different *isnad*, is called a *shahid* ("witness").[86]

2. *Afrad* (singular narrations).
3. The type of character required in an acceptable reporter.
4. The way a Hadith is heard, and the different ways of acquiring *Ahadith*.
5. How a Hadith is written, and punctuation marks used.
6. The way a Hadith is reported.
7. The manners required in traditionists.
8. The manners required in students of Hadith.
9. Knowledge of a higher or lower *isnad* (i.e. one with less or more reporters respectively).
10. Knowledge of difficult words.
11. Knowledge of abrogated *Ahadith*.
12. Knowledge of altered words in a text or *isnad*.
13. Knowledge of contradictory *Ahadith*.
14. Knowledge of additions made to an *isnad* (i.e. by an inserting the name of an additional reporter).
15. Knowledge of a well-concealed type of *mursal* Hadith.
16. Knowledge of the Companions.
17. Knowledge of the Successors.
18. Knowledge of elders reporting from younger reporters.
19. Knowledge of reporters similar in age reporting from each other.
20. Knowledge of brothers and sisters among reporters.
21. Knowledge of fathers reporting from their sons.
22. Knowledge of sons reporting from their fathers.
23. Knowledge of cases where e.g. two reporters report from the same authority, one in his early life and the other in his old age; in such cases the dates of death of the two reporters will be of significance.

---

[86] *Ibid*, p. 156.

24. Knowledge of such authorities from whom only one person reported.

25. Knowledge of such reporters who are known by a number of names and titles.

26. Knowledge of unique names amongst the Companions in particular and the reporters in general.

27. Knowledge of names and by-names (*kunyah*).

28. Knowledge of by-names for reporters known by their names only.

29. Knowledge of nicknames (*alqab*) of the traditionists.

30. Knowledge of *mu'talif* and *mukhtalif* (names written similarly but pronounced differently), e.g. Kuraiz and Kariz.

31. Knowledge of *muttafiq* and *muftariq* (similar names but different identities), e.g. "Hanafi": there are two reporters who are called by this name; one because of his tribe Banu Hanifah; the other because of his attribution to a particular *madhhab* (school of thought in jurisprudence).

32. Names covering both the previous types.

33. Names looking similar but they differ because of the difference in their father's names, e.g. Yazid b. al-Aswad and al-Aswad b. Yazid.

34. Names attributed to other than their fathers, e.g. Isma'il b. Umayyah; in this case Umayyah is the mother's name.

35. Knowledge of such titles which have a meaning different from what they seem to be, e.g. Abu Mas'ud al-Badri, not because he witnessed the battle of Badr but because he came to live there; Mu'awiyah b. 'Abdul Karim al-Dall ("the one going astray"), not because of his beliefs but because he lost his way while travelling to Makkah; and 'Abdullah b. Muhammad al-Da'if ("the weak"), not because of his reliability in Hadith, but due to a weak physique.

36. Knowledge of ambiguous reporters by finding out their names.

37. Knowledge of the dates of birth and death of reporters.

38. Knowledge of trustworthy and weak reporters.

39. Knowledge of trustworthy reporters who became confused in their old age.
40. Knowledge of contemporaries in a certain period.
41. Knowledge of free slaves (*mawali*) amongst the reporters.
42. Knowledge of the homelands and home towns of reporters.[87]

---

[87] See *Muqaddimah Ibn al-Salah.*

APPENDIX:
Verdicts on the *Ahadith* mentioned in the Foreword

1. *Mutawatir*, as declared by many scholars, including Ibn Taimiyyah, al-Suyuti, Najm al-Din al-Iskandari (d. 981) and al-'Ijlouni (d. 1162). About this Hadith, al-Daraqutni said, "It is the most authentic one regarding the virtues of any *surah*." It is related by al-Bukhari, Muslim and others.

2. The following is the *sahih* Hadith of al-Bukhari, Muslim, al-Tirmidhi, Ibn Majah and Ibn 'Asakir: "Verily, Allah has Ninety-Nine Names which if a person safeguards them, he will enter the Garden." In some narrations of this Hadith found in al-Tirmidhi, Ibn Majah, al-Hakim and others, the names are listed at the end; however, at least three different listings are given, e.g. one list being, "He is Allah, besides whom there is no other deity, the Merciful, the Compassionate, ..., the Forbearing" while another is "Allah, the Unique, the Absolute, ..., the One who has nothing like unto Him." It is agreed that these latter narrations are *da'if*, and this is why al-Bukhari and Muslim did not include them in their *Sahihs*. Al-Tirmidhi says in his *Sunan*, "This (version of the) Hadith is *gharib*; it has been narrated from various routes on the authority of Abu Hurairah, but we do not know of the mention of the Names in the numerous narrations, except this one."

Ibn Taimiyyah says, "Al-Walid (one of the narrators of the Hadith) related the Names from (the saying of) one of his Syrian teachers ... specific mention of the Names is not from the words of the Prophet ﷺ, by the agreement of those familiar with Hadith."[88] Ibn Kathir says in his *Tafsir*, under verse 180 of Surah al-A'raf, that these narrations are *mudraj*. Ibn Hajar takes a similar view in his commentary on *Sahih al-Bukhari*. Various scholars have given different lists of 99 Names from their study of the Qur'an and Sunnah, including Ja'far al- Sadiq, Sufyan b. 'Uyainah, Ibn Hazm, al-Qurtubi, Ibn Hajar and Salih b. 'Uthaimin.

3. Ibn Taimiyyah says, "It is not from the words of the Prophet ﷺ, and there is no known *isnad* for it, neither *sahih* nor *da'if*'; al-Zarkashi (d. 794), Ibn Hajar, al-Suyuti and others agreed with him. Al-Qari says, "But its meaning is correct, deduced from the statement of Allah, I have not created the Jinn and Mankind, except to worship Me, i.e. to recognise/know me, as Ibn 'Abbas ﷺ has explained." These statements are mentioned by al-'Ijlouni, who adds, "This saying occurs often in the words of the Sufis, who have relied on it and built upon it some of their principles."[89]

4. Al-'Ijlouni says, "Al-Saghani (d. 650) said: *Maudu'*. I say: But its meaning is correct, even if it is not a Hadith." no. 2123. 'Ali al- Qari says, "But its meaning is correct, for al-Dailami has related from Ibn 'Abbas as *marfu'*: 'that Jibril came to me and said: O Muhammad! Were it not for you, the Garden would not have been created, and were it not for you, the Fire would not have been created', and in the narration of Ibn 'Asakir: 'Were it not for you, the world would not have been created'." Al-Albani also quotes al-Saghani's verdict, and comments on al-Qari's words thus, "It is not appropriate to certify the correctness of its meaning without establishing the authenticity of the narration from al-Dailami, which is something I have not found any of the scholars to have addressed. Personally, although I have not come across its *isnad*, I have no doubt about its weakness; enough of an indication for us is that al-Dailami is alone in reporting it. As for the narration of Ibn 'Asakir, Ibn al-Jauzi also related it in a long *marfu'* Hadith

---

[88] *Fatawa Ibn Taimiyyah*, 6:379-382.
[89] Isma'il b. Muhammad al-'Ijlouni, *Kashf al- Khafa'* (2 vols. in 1, Cairo/Aleppo, N.D.), no. 2016.

from Salman and said, 'It is *maudu'*, and al-Suyuti endorsed this in *al-La'ali*."[90]

5. *Sahih* - related by al-Bukhari and Muslim.

6. Al-'Ijlouni says, "Al-Ghazali mentioned it in *Ihya' 'Ulum al-Din* with the wording, Allah says, "Neither My heaven nor My earth could contain Me, but the soft, humble heart of my believing slave can contain Me." Al-'Iraqi said in his notes on *al-Ihya'*, "I do not find a basis (i.e. *isnad*) for it", and al-Suyuti agreed with him, following al-Zarkashi. Al-'Iraqi then said, "But in the Hadith of Abu 'Utbah in al-Tabarani there occurs: ... the vessels of your Lord are the hearts of His righteous slaves, and the most beloved to Him are the softest and most tender ones." Ibn Taimiyyah said, "It is mentioned in the Israelite traditions, but there is no known *isnad* from the Prophet ﷺ for it." Al-Sakhawi said in *al-Maqasid*, following his shaykh al-Suyuti in *al- La'ali*, "There is no known *isnad* from the Prophet ﷺ for it, and its meaning is that his heart can contain belief in Me, love of Me and gnosis of Me. But as for the one who says that Allah incarnates in the hearts of the people, then he is more of an infidel than the Christians, who specified that to Christ alone. It seems that Ibn Taimiyyah's mention of Israelite tradition refers to what Ahmad has related in Al-Zuhd from Wahb b. Munabbih who said that Allah opened the heavens for Ezekiel until he saw the Throne, so Ezekiel said, 'How Perfect are You! How Mighty are You, O Lord!' So Allah said, 'Truly, the heavens and the earth were too weak to contain Me, but the soft, humble heart of my believing slave contains Me'." He also quoted from al-Zarkashi's writing that one of the scholars said that it is a false Hadith, fabricated by a renegade (from the religion), and that it is most-often quoted by a preacher to the masses, 'Ali b. Wafa, for his own purposes, who says at the time of spiritual rapture and dance, "Go round the House of your Lord." He further said that al-Tabarani has related from Abu 'Utbah al-Khawlani as *marfu'*, "Truly, Allah has vessels from amongst the people of

---

[90] Al-Albani, *Silsilah al-Ahadith al-Da'ifah*, no. 282.

the earth, and the vessels of your Lord are the hearts of his righteous slaves, and the most beloved of them to Him are the softest and most tender ones"; in its *isnad* is Baqiyyah b. al-Walid, a mudallis, but he has clearly stated hearing the Hadith."[91]   Al-Albani rates this last Hadith mentioned as *hasan*.[92]

7. Al-Nawawi said, "It is not established." Ibn Taimiyyah said, "*Maudu'*." Al-Sam'ani said, "It is not known as *marfu'*, but it is quoted as a statement of Yahya b. Mu'adh al-Razi." Al- Suyuti endorsed al-Nawawi's words, and also said, "This Hadith is not authentic." Al-Fairozabadi said, "It is not a Prophetic statement, although most of the people think it is a Hadith, but it is not authentic at all. In fact, it is only related in the Israelite traditions: O Man! Know yourself: you will know your Lord." Ibn al-Gharas said, after quoting al-Nawawi's verdict, "... but the books of the Sufis, such as Shaykh Muhi al-Din Ibn 'Arabi and others, are filled with it, being quoted like a Hadith." Ibn 'Arabi also said, "This Hadith, although it is not proved by way of narration, is proved to us by way of *kashf* ('unveiling', while in a trance)."[93]

Regarding this methodology, al-Albani says, "Authenticating Ahadith by way of *kashf* is a wicked innovation of the Sufis, and depending upon it leads to the authentication of false, baseless *Ahadith* ... This is because, even at the best of times, *kashf* is like opinion, which may be right or wrong - and that is if no personal desires enter into it! We ask Allah to save us from it, and from everything with which He is not pleased."[94]

8. *Sahih*. Related by Malik in *al-Muwatta'*, al- Shafi'i in *al-Risalah* (p. 110, Eng. trans.) and Muslim (1:382; Eng. trans. 1:272). This was the first of two questions which the Prophet ﷺ put to a slave-girl to test her faith, the second one being, "Who am I?" She answered, "Above the heaven" and "You

---

[91] *Kashf al-Khafa'*, no. 2256.

[92] *Sahih al-Jami' al-Saghir*, no. 2163; *Silsilah al-Ahadith al-Sahihah*, no. 1691.

[93] *Kashf al-Khafa'*, no. 2532; *Al-Da'ifah*, no. 66.

[94] *Al-Da'ifah*, no. 58.

are the Messenger of Allah" respectively, to which he said, "Free her, for she is a believer." Her first answer, which is found in the Qur'an (67:16-17, the word fi can mean 'above/on', as in 6:11, 20:71 & 27:8), means that Allah is above and separate from His creation, not mixed in with it, the erroneous belief which leads to worship of creation.

9. *Maudu'*, as stated by al-Saghani and others. Scholars differ as to whether its meaning is correct or not, in what way, and to what extent.[95] It is sometimes used to justify divisive, anti-Islamic nationalism and patriotism!

10. *Sahih.* Related by Malik as *mursal/mu'allaq/balaghat* (depending on choice of terminology), and related twice as *musnad* by al-Hakim. The meaning of the Hadith is contained in the Qur'an, in the mention of the Book and Wisdom (2:129, 2:151, 2:231, 3:164, 4:113, 33:34 & 62:2); al-Shafi'i says, "I have heard the most knowledgeable people about the Qur'an say that the Wisdom is the Sunnah" (*al-Risalah*, Eng. trans., p. 111).

11. *Sahih.* Related by al-Tirmidhi, Ahmad, Ibn Abi 'Asim, al-Hakim, al-Tabarani, al-Dailami and al-Tahawi.[96] The phrase Ahl al-Bayt (members of the house) refers: (i) primarily to the Prophet's wives ﷺ, from the clear context of the relevant verse of the Qur'an (33:33); (ii) to 'Ali, Fatimah, Hasan & Husain, from the "Hadith of the garment" (cf. *Sahih Muslim*, Book of the Virtues of the Companions). It is imbalanced and unjust to exclude either of these categories from the Hadith.

12. A *sahih* Hadith related by Abu Dawud, al-Tirmidhi, Ibn Majah & Ahmad, and well-known amongst the people. The fullest narration is, "Abu Bakr will be in the Garden; 'Umar will be in the Garden; 'Uthman will be in the Garden; 'Ali will be in the Garden; Talhah will be in the Garden; al-Zubair will be in the Garden; 'Abd al-Rahman b. 'Auf will be in the Garden;

---

[95] *Kashf al-Khafa'*, no. 1102; *Al-Da'ifah*, no. 36.
[96] *Al-Sahihah*, no. 1761.

Sa'd b. Abi Waqqas will be in the Garden; Sa'id b. Zaid will be in the Garden; Abu 'Ubaidah b. al-Jarrah will be in the Garden."

13. Related by Ishaq b. Rahawaih and al-Baihaqi with a *sahih isnad* as a statement of 'Umar. It is also collected by Ibn 'Adi and al-Dailami from Ibn 'Umar as *marfu'*, but in its *isnad* is 'Isa b. Abdullah, who is weak. However, it is strengthened by another narration of Ibn 'Adi, and also supported by the Hadith in the *Sunan* that a man saw in a dream that Prophet ﷺ was weighed against Abu Bakr, and was found to be heavier; then Abu Bakr was weighed against everyone else...[97]

14. Related by al-Hakim, al-Tabarani and others. It is also related by al-Tirmidhi with the wording, "I am the House of Wisdom, and 'Ali is its Door". Al-Daraqutni labelled the Hadith as *mudtarib*, both in *isnad* and text; al-Tirmidhi said it is *gharib* and *munkar*; al-Bukhari said that it has no *sahih* narration; Ibn Ma'in said that it is a baseless lie. Similar dismissals of the Hadith are reported from Abu Zur'ah, Abu Hatim and Yahya b. Sa'd. Al-Hakim declared the original Hadith as *sahih* in *isnad*, but Ibn al-Jauzi regarded both versions as *maudu'*, and al-Dhahabi agreed with him. Several of the later scholars, including Ibn Hajar al-'Asqalani, Ibn Hajar al-Makki and al-Suyuti declared it *hasan* due to its various routes of narration. Al-'Ijlouni says, "... none of this devalues the consensus of the Adherents to the Sunnah from the Companions, the Successors and those after them, that the best of the Companions overall is Abu Bakr, followed by 'Umar ...", and quotes this view from Ibn 'Umar and 'Ali himself, as recorded in *Sahih al-Bukhari*.[98] Al-Albani declares the Hadith to be *maudu'*.[99]

15. A *da'if* or *maudu'* Hadith, as stated by Ahmad b. Hanbal, Ibn 'Abd al-Barr, al-Bazzar and many others. Ibn Hazm states that not only is the *isnad* unsound, but the Hadith cannot be true for two further reasons: (i)

---

[97] *Kashf al-Khafa'*, no. 2130.
[98] *Kashf al-Khafa'*, no. 618.
[99] *Da'if al-Jami' al-Saghir*, nos. 1410, 1416.

the Companions were not infallible, and hence made mistakes, so it would be wrong to say that following any of them leads to guidance; (ii) the comparison with the stars is wrong, for not every star guides one through every journey! There is a different, authentic comparison with the stars given in *Sahih Muslim*: the Prophet ﷺ said, "The stars are the custodians of the sky, so when the stars depart, there will come to the sky what is promised for it (i.e. on the Day of Judgment). I am the custodian of my Companions, so when I depart, there will come to my Companions what is promised for them (i.e. great trials and tribulations). My Companions are the custodians for my *Ummah*, so when my Companions depart, there will come to my *Ummah* what is promised for it (i.e. schisms, spread of innovations, etc.)." (4:1961, Eng. trans. IV:1344)

16. No *isnad* exists for this Hadith: al-Subki (d. 756) said, "It is not known to the scholars of Hadith, and I cannot find an *isnad* for it, whether *sahih, da'if,* or *maudu'*." It, along with the previous one, is often used to justify the following two extremes: (i) blind following of the views of men, with no reference to the Qur'an and Sunnah; (ii) conveniently following whichever scholar holds the easiest view, or that most agreeable to one's desires, again without reference to the fundamental sources.

17. Numerous narrations of this Hadith are found in the collections of Abu Dawud, al-Tirmidhi, Ibn Majah, al-Hakim, Ahmad and others: they vary in being *sahih, hasan,* or *da'if,* but the Hadith is established. Among those who have authenticated this Hadith are al-Tirmidhi, al-Hakim, al-Shatibi, Ibn Taimiyyah, Ibn al-Qayyim, al-Dhahabi, Ibn Kathir, Ibn Hajar and al-'Iraqi. Most narrations mention the splitting-up of the Jews and the Christians into seventy-one or seventy-two sects, all being in the Fire except one, prior to mention of the Muslims dividing even more. In some of the narrations, the Prophet ﷺ describes the Saved Sect variously as "the *Jama'ah* (community, congregation, main body)", "the largest body (*al-sawad al-a'zam*)" and "that which follows what I and my Companions are upon."

The Hadith does not mean that the majority of Muslims will be in the Hellfire, for most of them ("the masses") are not involved in intentional, divisive innovation; further, mention of the Fire does not necessarily imply that the seventy-two sects will remain there forever, or that those sects are disbelievers.

18. Although the Mahdi is not mentioned explicitly in the collections of al-Bukhari and Muslim, numerous *sahih Ahadith*, which are *mutawatir* in meaning, speak of the coming of the Mahdi, a man named Muhammad b. 'Abdullah and a descendant of the Prophet ﷺ through Fatimah, who will be the Leader (Imam, *Khalifah*) of the Muslims, rule for seven years and fill the world with justice and equity after it had been filled with tyranny and oppression. He will also fight the Dajjal along with Jesus son of Mary. The author, in his The Concept of the Mahdi among the Ahl al-Sunnah, has named 37 scholars who collected *Ahadith* about the Mahdi with their own isnads and 69 later scholars who wrote in support of the concept, compared to 8 scholars who rejected the idea.

The *Ahadith* prophesying the Dajjal (False Christ), a one-eyed man who will have miraculous powers and will be followed by the Jews, and the return of Jesus Christ son of Mary (peace be upon them), who will descend in Damascus and pray behind the Mahdi, kill the Dajjal at the gate of Lod in Palestine, break the Cross, kill the Pig, marry and have children and live for forty years before dying a natural death, are *mutawatir* in meaning. They have been collected by al-Bukhari and Muslim, as well as other traditionists.

19. *Mutawatir* in meaning, and collected by al-Bukhari, Muslim and others.

20. *Mutawatir* in meaning, and collected by al- Bukhari, Muslim and others. Mention of the inadmissibility of intercession on the Day of Judgment in the Qur'an, e.g. 2:48 2:123, must be understood in the light of other verses, e.g. 20:109 and *sahih Ahadith*. The reward of seeing Allah for

the believers is referred to in the Qur'an, e.g. 75:22-23 and 83:15. These *Ahadith* and those of the previous two categories were generally rejected by the classical *Mu'tazilah* (Rationalists), as well by those influenced by them today, on one or more of the following bases: (i) they contradict the Qur'an (in their view); (ii) they contradict Reason (in their view), and (iii) they are *ahad*, not *mutawatir*, and hence not acceptable in matters of belief (a flawed argument). Hence, the scholars who wrote the *'aqidah* (creed) of the Ahl al-Sunnah included these concepts in it, to confirm their denial of the wrong ideas of the *Mu'tazilah*. Other authentic *Ahadith* rejected by the *Mu'tazilah* are many, and include those describing the Prophet's *Mi'raj* (ascension to the heavens), which are again *mutawatir* in meaning.

21. The Hadith with this wording is *da'if*, but its meaning is contained in the Hadith of Ibn Majah and al-Nasa'i that a man came to the Prophet ﷺ and said, "O Messenger of Allah! I intend to go on a (military) expedition, but I have come to ask your advice." He said, "Is your mother alive?" He said, "Yes." He said, "Then stay with her, for the Garden is under her feet." This latter Hadith is declared to be *sahih* by al-Hakim, al-Dhahabi and al-Mundhiri.[100]

22. A *sahih* Hadith, collected by al-Bukhari, Muslim and others.

23. This Hadith has many chains of narration on the authority of more than a dozen Companions, including twenty Successors apparently reporting from Anas alone. They are collected by Ibn Majah, al-Baihaqi, al-Tabarani and others, but all of them are *da'if*, according to Ahmad b. Hanbal, Ishaq b. Rahuwaih, Ibn 'Abd al-Barr, al-Bazzar and others, although some scholars authenticated a few of the chains. Al-Baihaqi said that its text is *mashhur* while its *isnad* is *da'if*, while al-Hakim and Ibn al-Salah regarded it as a prime example of a *mashhur* Hadith which is not *sahih*. However, it is regarded by later scholars of Hadith as having enough chains

---

[100] *Kashf al-Khafa'*, no. 1078; *Al-Da'ifah*, no. 593.

of narration to be strengthened to the level of *hasan* or *sahih*, a view which is stated by al- Mizzi, al-'Iraqi, Ibn Hajar, al-Suyuti and al-Albani.[101]

24. This additional statement is found in a few of the (weak) narrations of the previous Hadith, and is declared as *maudu'* by Ibn Hibban, Ibn al-Jauzi, al-Sakhawi and al-Albani.[102]

25. Mentioned by al-Manjaniqi in his collection of *Ahadith* of older narrators reporting from younger ones, on the authority of al-Hasan al-Basri. Al-Khatib al-Baghdadi said that it is *maudu'* as a narration from the Prophet ﷺ, but that it is a statement of al-Hasan al-Basri.[103]

26. Related as *marfu'* by al-Baihaqi with a *da'if isnad*, according to al-'Iraqi. Ibn Hajar said that it is actually a saying of Ibrahim b. Abi 'Ablah, a Successor.[104]

*NB: The scholars of Hadith agree that a *da'if* or *maudu'* Hadith must not be attributed to the Prophet ﷺ, e.g. by saying, "The Prophet said: ...", even if the meaning is considered to be correct or if it is actually the saying of a Muslim scholar, for that would be a way of lying about the Prophet ﷺ.

---

[101] *Kashf al-Khafa'*, no. 1665; *Sahih al-Jami' al- Saghir*, nos. 3913-4.
[102] *Al-Da'ifah*, no. 416; *Da'if al-Jami' al-Saghir*, nos. 1005-6.
[103] *Kashf al-Khafa'*, no. 2276.
[104] *Kashf al-Khafa'*, no. 1362.

Supplement to *An Introduction to the Science of Hadith*

This supplement is divided into two parts. The first is mainly devoted to the Knowledge of *AI-Jarh wa al-Ta'dil* (Disparaging and Authenticating). It covers many points in detail that were briefly discussed in the book, as well as a number of new topics such as:

i.   The Knowledge of the Companions and the Successors.

ii.   The Knowledge regarding the age recognized for receiving the Hadith and delivering it.

iii.   The methods through which Hadith were received and imparted.

In Part Two, all remaining branches of Knowledge as mentioned in Section C of the book are taken in detail. Only those that are covered in part One are not repeated.

PART ONE

The knowledge of hadith mainly covers two branches:

A. The Knowledge related to the narration of Hadith (*al-Riwaya*). This deals with narrating the words of Hadith accurately, gathering together the various *isnad* and determining the names of each of the reporters.

B. The Knowledge related to finding out a ruling about the Hadith (*al-Diraya*). This deals with scrutinizing the state of the reporter and the text of the Hadith in order to reach a verdict as to whether it is acceptable or not.

By this definition of *al-Diraya*, we can say that the knowledge of the science of Hadith (*Usul al-Hadith*) is the one concerned with *al-Diraya*. We have also come to know that the knowledge of the terms discussed in the Science of Hadith aims at finding the final verdict about a Hadith which may be as 'sahih' (sound), 'hasan' (good), 'da'if' (weak) or 'maudu' (invented). All other terms rotate around these four. In this study, we are concerned with how all these terms pave the way towards reaching the final objective.

A Hadith consists of a text (*matn*) and the chain of reporters (*isnad*) who happened to narrate it. The first narrator of a Hadith must be a Companion (*Sahabi*) from whom a Successor (*Tabi'i*) narrates. Unless a Hadith finds its place in one of the famous collections (like those of Imam Malik, Bukhari and Muslim), it may pass through some further reporters. Thus, it is imperative to find about the credibility of each reporter as far as his general state of trustworthiness (*thiqa*) and the preservation of the words (*dabt*). Therefore the first step in scrutinizing a Hadith is the knowledge about a Companion.

1. Knowledge about a Companion

According, to the traditionists, a *Sahabi* is the one who met the Prophet ﷺ in the state of Islam and died in the state of Islam as well. He could be traced as a *Sahabi* through any of the following:

- He had been mentioned in the Qur'an, like Abu Bakr Al-Siddiq (*Surah al-Tauba*: 40) and Zayd (*Surah al-Ahzab*: 37)
- By way of *tawatur* - like the ten who were given the good news of entering into Paradise by the Prophet ﷺ.
- Reputed famously to be a *Sahabi* - like Thabit bin Qais, Dhul Yadain etc.
- Witnessed by another *Sahabi* to be a Companion - like 'Ukkasha bin Mihsan, who was mentioned by Abdullah b Abbas in his Hadith.
- Through the narration directly from the Prophet ﷺ.
- Witnessed by a reliable Successor to be a *Sahabi*.
- He claims to be a *Sahabi* and had been known as a trustworthy person.

As far as the Companions are concerned, they are considered to be 'trustworthy' as Allah Almighty mentioned them in the Qur'an with praiseworthy remarks. e.g. He said about the early emigrants and those who helped them in Madinah:

﴿ وَٱلسَّٰبِقُونَ ٱلْأَوَّلُونَ مِنَ ٱلْمُهَٰجِرِينَ وَٱلْأَنصَارِ وَٱلَّذِينَ ٱتَّبَعُوهُم بِإِحْسَٰنٍ رَّضِىَ ٱللَّهُ عَنْهُمْ وَرَضُواْ عَنْهُ وَأَعَدَّ لَهُمْ جَنَّٰتٍ تَجْرِى تَحْتَهَا ٱلْأَنْهَٰرُ خَٰلِدِينَ فِيهَآ أَبَدًا ذَٰلِكَ ٱلْفَوْزُ ٱلْعَظِيمُ ﴾

"**The vanguard of Islam – the first of those who forsook their homes and of those who gave them aid, and also those who follow them in all good deeds - Well-pleased is God with**

them, as they are with Him; for them hath He prepared gardens under which rivers flow, to dwell therein forever, that is the supreme Felicity." (9:100)

This also covers all the other Companions because they are the ones who followed them.

He praised in particular those who gave the Prophet ﷺ the oath of allegiance under the tree at Hudaibiya, at the outskirts of Makkah in the 6th year of Hijra:

﴿ لَّقَدْ رَضِيَ ٱللَّهُ عَنِ ٱلْمُؤْمِنِينَ إِذْ يُبَايِعُونَكَ تَحْتَ ٱلشَّجَرَةِ فَعَلِمَ مَا فِي قُلُوبِهِمْ فَأَنزَلَ ٱلسَّكِينَةَ عَلَيْهِمْ وَأَثَبَهُمْ فَتْحًا قَرِيبًا ﴾

"God's good pleasure was on the believers when they swore fealty to thee under the tree; He knew what was in their hearts, and he sent down tranquillity to them, and He rewarded them with a speedy victory." (48:18)

Allah's pleasure with the Companions in general is shown in verse 122 of *Surah Al-Ma'idah*, verse 22 of *Surah Al-Mujadilah* and verse 8 of *Surah Al-Bayyinah*.

Thus as long as all the Companions are trustworthy, is there a need to find out about their biographies?

The answer is in the affirmative. This is because there may be some who are confused with the Companions while they in reality are not from amongst them. This vital need led to the compilation of a number of books, all related to the names of the Companions, men and women, with brief or detailed sketches about their life history. These types of books are known to be related to the knowledge of the layers or groups of people (*al-Tabaqat*). The benefits that can be derived from these books are as follows:

i. To find out whether a reporter is a Companion or a Successor. For example, Hujr bin Adi who was killed by Caliph Mu'awiya had been a centre of this discussion. By reading his life history and examining different reports about him, this study led us to determine that he was not a Companion and that Mu'awiya should not be held responsible for killing a Companion. The events that led to his killing could also be traced in such a Study.[105]

ii. To know about the junior Companions who would be most likely to report most of their narratives through elder Companions.

iii. To differentiate between the sayings of the Companions (entitled as *mauquf*) from those of the Prophet ﷺ (known as *'marfu'*).

Among the most famous books about this knowledge are the following:

- *Al-Isti'ab fi Ma'rifat al-Ashab* by ibn Abdul Barr (d. 463AH).
- *Usud ul Ghaba* by Izz ul-Din Ibn Al-Athir (d. 606AH).
- *Al-Isabah fi Tamyiz Al-Sahabah* by Ibn Hajar Al-Asqalani. This book listed 10741 men and 1552 women among the Companions.

2. Discussion about receiving the Hadith (*tahammul*) and imparting it (*ada'*)

A part of this discussion is devoted to the knowledge of the junior Companions to find out whether the recipient of the Hadith was intelligent enough to remember what he heard. For this purpose no specific time of age is set except that the person must have reached the age of discerning (*tamyiz*), i.e. that he can understand the question and answer it properly.

---

[105] *Al-Awasim min Al-Qawasim*, by Ibn Al-Arabi.

For example, a very junior Companion named Mahmud bin Al-Rubayyi reported that the Prophet ﷺ once gargled and spat water on his face. He was just five years old at that time.[106] The important factor is that the ability of the child of that age to understand and comprehend. It may be the age of five for some, more or less for some others as the children differ in intelligence.

However, the traditionists agree to accept that Hadith from the child after he reaches the age of majority. This means the age at which a Hadith could be delivered by a child is the age of attaining his adulthood. On the mode of delivering the Hadith (*sighat al-ada'*), we will speak under number 13 of this study.

This knowledge helps to determine whether a junior's report should be accepted or not.

3. Scrutinizing the authenticity of Hadith among the Companions

The following examples show that the scrutinizing of Hadith was not a feature of later times but it had been known among, the Companions as well.

i. 'Urwa bin Zubair reported that 'Aisha said to him: "O my nephew! It reached me that Abdullah bin Amr is going to come for Hajj, so visit him and ask him as he has carried a lot of knowledge from the Prophet ﷺ."

So he narrated from him a number of Ahadith including this one:

> **"Allah does not snatch the knowledge from the people (abruptly) but by taking the souls of the scholars. The knowledge is lifted away with them. Only some ignorant people are left behind who give rulings on different issues**

---

[106] *Sahih Al-Bukhari.*

and (because of ignorance) they mislead the people and are misled themselves."

Urwah said: "When I related this Hadith to 'Aisha, she took it very seriously but did not recognize it (as a Hadith) and said: 'Are you sure that he told you that he heard it from the Prophet ﷺ?' Urwah said: The following year, 'Aisha asked me to visit him on his arrival again and to ask him about this particular Hadith. Urwah then said: So I met him and asked him about that Hadith and he narrated it to me the same as he narrated it last year, I came to 'Aisha and reported to her, She said: 'I think he is right and truthful as he neither added to what he said previously nor deleted any of its words'."[107]

ii. Abu Musa Al-Ash'ari reported that he came to visit Umar. As according to Sunnah, he said *'A-Salam 'Alaikum'* three times loudly at his door. When he received no response, he started coming back. Umar came out and shouted to Abu Musa asking him why he was retreating. He told him that this was the Sunnah for a visitor. Umar was furious and asked for a witness for what he had claimed. Worried and frightened, Abu Musa came to the mosque and asked the people if any of them could corroborate his statement. They said: 'The youngest among us is going to bear witness for you'. By this they meant Abu Sa'id Al-Khudri, who stood up and stated to Umar that he had heard it from the Prophet ﷺ. Umar thus did not reject the Hadith, but what he wanted was that people exercised more care when they narrated the Hadith of the Prophet ﷺ. He said to Abu Musa: "I am not accusing you but I feared that people might attribute things wrongly to the Prophet ﷺ."[108]

The same could be said about Ali when he would ask the reporters to take an oath in the name or Allah before narrating a Hadith.

This type of knowledge shows how important the Science of Hadith is and how greatly it is needed for a student of Hadith.

---

[107] *Sahih Muslim, Kitab ul-Ilm.*
[108] *Ma'rifat al-Sunan wa al-Athar, 1:32.*

4. The knowledge about a Successor

A Successor is the one who happened to see a Companion and listened to him. By knowing them, one can differentiate between a *mauquf* and *maqtu'* narration. It also helps to differentiate between a *mursall* Hadith of a Companion and that of a Successor.

The Successors are normally categorized in three sections: elder, middle and junior. We have already said in our discussion about *mursal* Hadith that the *mursal* of the elder Successors are more likely to be accepted because they happened to take it from a Companion, unlike a junior Successor who might have also taken the Hadith from another Successor. By knowing them we can also avoid the reports of the weak among them, such as al-Harith Al-A'war, Mukhtar Al-Thaqafi and Asim bin Damurah.

Take a look at what the traditionists note about each one of them:

i. Al-Harith b. Abdullah At-Hamdani Al-A'war: Among the renowned scholars of successors with weakness in him. All four books of *Sunan* report from him. He is declared weak and a liar by Al-Sha'bi and Ali b. Al-Madini. Ibn Hibban said: 'Al-Harith was extreme in his following of Shi'ism'.[109]

ii. Al-Mukhtar b Abi 'Ubaid Al-Thaqafi: The Liar. No one should report from him because he was misleading and a deviant. He claimed that Angel Jibrail used to visit him.

iii. Asim b. Damurah: Among the companions of Ali. All four Sunan books report from him. Imam Ahmed said: "He is higher than Al-Harith Al-A'war. He is reliable to me". He is declared trustworthy by both Ibn Ma'in and Ibn al-Madini. However, Ibn Adi said: "He is the source of all troubles".[110]

---

[109] *Mizan Al-'Itidal* 1:435-437.
[110] *Mizan*, 2:352.

For the life sketches of the Successors, the following books would be very helpful:

- *Tabaqat* by Ibn Sa'd, the volume on the Successors.
- *Mizan al-I'tidal* by Ibn Hajar.

5. Pre-requisite for a *sahih* Hadith

The definition of a *sahih* Hadith covers five conditions as has been discussed in the Science of Hadith. To expand on them further, let us examine the states of character the reporter needs to have:

i.   Islam
ii.   To be adult
iii. Sanity of mind
iv.   Devoid of sins and such characteristics which are repugnant to manly behaviour
v.   Carefulness in narration
      Good memory if he reports from memory and good understanding if he reports the meanings of Hadith (as opposed to the exact wording).[111]

To explain some prominent features of these conditions further:

i) Islam

The narration of a non-believer is not acceptable because his infidelity is lower than a sinful person (Fasiq) whose testimony is rejected in Islam.

ii) Adulthood (the age of *taklif*)

---

[111] Ibn Kathir, *Al-Ba'ith Al-Hathith*, p 92.

A child is not expected to comprehend the consequences of a lie or mistake when narrating a Hadith. This is why his report is not accepted but after adulthood. As for receiving it, the age of discerning, as earlier discussed is acceptable. Among such minor Companions whose reports were accepted at the age of majority were Abdullah b. Abbas, Abdullah b. Zubayr, Nu'man b. Bashir and others.

iii) Being reliable (*adil*), on the contrary to being sinful (*fasiq*)

According to Ibn Hibban a man is reliable as long as he shows obedience to Allah Almighty in the majority of the time, as there is never a person who did not commit a sin.[112]

According to Al-Hakim, a reliable person is the one who does not call other people to an innovation which he happened to do, and does not sin publically so as to lose face amongst the people.[113]

As for manly characters (*muru'a*), the most comprehensive definition comes from Ali ibn Abi Talib. He reports from the Prophet ﷺ as saying: "Whoever treats the people without injustice, speaks to them without lies, promises them without failing, and is perfect in his manly characters. His reliability is apparent. He deserves to be treated like a brother and backbiting him is prohibited."[114]

"To some others, habits like eating while you walk, urinating in the path, accompanying mean and bad people, joking excessively etc. all stand as repugnant to manly characters. Anyhow, such unacceptable habits (as for traditionists) differ from place to place and people to people."[115]

iv) Preservation (*dabt*)

---

[112] *Sahih Ibn Hibban*, 1: 113.
[113] *Ulum Al-Hadith*, p 53.
[114] *Al-Kifaya* by Khatib al-Baghdadi, p 136.
[115] *Al-Mustasfa* by Al-Ghazali, 1:157.

A preserver (*dabit*) of Hadith is the one whose mistakes are found to be very few. The following conditions are required in a good preserver of Hadith:

a. Carefulness in reports, knowing what is right from what is wrong.

b. Sharpness in memory so that he does not fail to quote when needed.

c. Once his reports are preserved in a book, he protects it from any interpolation or change.

d. He comprehends the words so well that if he has to narrate the meanings of Hadith, he does not change the meaning at all.[116]

Let us now take a further three conditions of *sahih* Hadith separately.

6. Continuity of *isnad*

Any missing link in a chain of Hadith renders it to be abandoned unless that link is formed and proved to be reliable. During the time of the Successors, traditionists used to scrutinize each *isnad*, especially when it came from weak reporters. 'Utba b. Hakim reported that he was in the company of Ishaq b. Abi Farwah, he started saying: "The Messenger of Allah said so. The Messenger of Allah said so." Al-Zuhri shouted: "May Allah fight you! O lbn Abi Farwah! How dare you, are you against Allah? Cannot you give the *isnad* of your Hadith? You narrate to us *Ahadith* with no end or tail."[117]

Abu Ishaq Ibrahim b. Isa Al-Taliqani reported: "I said to Abdullah b. Al-Mubarak: O Abu Abdul Rahman, what about this Hadith: 'Out of piety is that you pray for your parents whenever you pray, and fast for them whenever you fast'? Abdullah said: "O Abu Ishaq! From whom? " I said: "From among, the Hadith of Shihab b. Khirash." He said: "Trustworthy is he, but from whom?" I said: "From Al-Hajjaj b. Dinar." He said: "Trustworthy as

---

[116] *Al-Kifaya*, p 136.
[117] *Ma'rifat Ulum Al-Hadith* by Al-Hakim, p 6.

well, from whom?" I said: "From the Prophet ﷺ." He said: "O Abu Ishaq! Between Hajjaj b. Dinar and the Prophet are miles of deserts where even the camels do fail to cross. But there is no dispute about giving charity (Sadaqa on behalf of a dead person)."[118]

It is necessary, for this purpose, to know the *shuyukh* (teachers) of a reporter as well as his pupils. By knowing the *Isnad* a *Muttasil* Hadith could be differentiated from *Ahadith* with broken *Isnad* like *Mursal, Mu'dal, Munqati'* and *Mu'allaq*. See the diagrams for all these five categories:

a. Muttasil   Malik

⇩

Nafi'

⇩

Ibn Umar

⇩

The Prophet ﷺ

b. Mursal   Said b. Al-.Musayyab (Successor)

⇩

(Sahabi)

⇩

The Prophet ﷺ

c. Mu'dal   Imam Malik

⇩

(Successor)

⇩

(Sahabi)

⇩

The Prophet ﷺ

---

[118] *Sahih Muslim, Al-Muqaddima.*

d. Mu'allaq

Imam Bukhari

⇩

(missing link)

⇩

Malik

⇩

Zaid b. Aslam

⇩

Ata b. Yasar

⇩

Abu Said Al-Khudri

⇩

The Prophet ﷺ

e. Munqati'

Abu Amr Uthman b. Ahmad Al-Sammak

⇩

Abu Ayyub b. Sulaiman Al-Sa'di

⇩

Abdul Aziz b. Musa Abu Ruh

⇩

Hilal b Haqq

⇩

Al-Jariri

⇩

Abul Ala Ibn Al-Shikir

⇩

Two men From Banu Hanzala

⇩

Shaddad b. Aus

⇩

The Prophet ﷺ

The *isnad* is broken because of the ambiguity of the two men from Banu Hanzala.[119]

7. To know the hidden cause (`*illah*)

Only a very well versed traditionist could detect such a hidden cause to an Isnad, which seems to be sound and accurate, but is proved to be otherwise due to that hidden cause.

For example, Imam Hakim in his *Mustadrak* claimed to have collected *Ahadith* missed by both Bukhari and Muslim while they meet their conditions of acceptance. A good example is that of the Hadith of Al-Zuhri and Hushaim. Both are trustworthy on their own. Bukhari and Muslim have given *Ahadith* through each of them separately, but not as Hushaim reporting from Al-Zuhri.

Why? Because Hushaim once met Al-Zuhri and took front him twenty Hadith on some papers. On his way back home he met one of his friends who wanted to see the papers. As soon as he showed them, a strong wind blew them away. Later Hushaim started narrating these *Ahadith* from his memory without preserving them perfectly. Thus, he happened to make mistakes regarding them.

By this, the condition of 'Preservation of Hadith' is lost. Thus Hushaim, who is trustworthy by himself, is rendered weak whenever he narrated from Al-Zuhri. This point was missed by Al-Hakim, who sometimes depends on the reporters of Bukhari and Muslim and accepts any Hadith coming from them without knowing such defects as above.[120]

---

[119] *Taujih Al-Nazar ila Usul al-Athar* by Tahir b. Salih b. Ahmad Al-Jaza'iri, p 167.
[120] *Al-Jarh wa Al-Ta'dil* by Abu Lubaba Husain, p 93.

Among the traditionists, Abdul Rahman b. Hatim Muhammad b. ldris Al-Razi is known with his exhaustive book *'Ilal al-Hadith*, in which he has given his verdict on a great number of Hadith through his skilled knowledge of the subject. It is reported that a learned person known with Fiqh asked Abu Hatim about certain Ahadith. In his reply, he said about some of them, "It is a mistake" or "The man is confused. He grafted one Hadith to the other", or "This is totally false", or "This is unrecognized (Munkar)," or "This is sound". The man said to him, "From where do you know this? Did the reporter tell you that this one is a lie and that one is a mistake?" Al-Razi said, "No, but I knew it," The man said, "Do you claim the knowledge of the unseen?" He said, "No, I do not". The man said, "What is your evidence on what you say?" He said, "You should ask others from among our companions. If we happen to agree, you will know that we are not saying something out of speculation."

So the man went to Abu Zur'a and asked him about these Ahadith and found him agreeing to what Al-Razi had said. So the man wondered how these two persons were in agreement without a prior mutual understanding. Abu Hatim said to him, "So now you know that we do not speculate". Then he said, "The evidence about the truthfulness about our verdict is: take a fake Dinar to a money changer. If he tells you that it is a fake one, you are going to question him by saying, 'Were you present when someone counterfeited it?' or 'Did the counterfeiter tell you that he made it?' He would certainly deny it. Thus, it is knowledge which Allah, the Glorified, has bestowed upon us. Similarly, if you take a real diamond and a fake one made of glass to a jeweler, he would recognize the real one from the artificial one. As for us, we know the authenticity of Hadith from the reliability of its reporters and from its wording, as the wording of the Prophet ﷺ is distinguished from others. We know that a Hadith is weak or unrecognized when it comes from an unreliable reporter who is found to be the only one to report it."[121]

8. *Shudhudh* (oddness) in the Hadith

The definition of al-Shafi'i for a *shadhdh* Hadith is the best from among the traditionists. Let us take two more definitions which differ slightly from that of al-Shafi'i.

Abu Ya'la Al-Khalill says: "*shadhdh* is the one which has only one *isnad*. If it comes from an unreliable source, the Hadith is rejected. But if it comes from a reliable one, no verdict is given about it and it is not used for argument. "

Al-Hakim takes a further step and says: "*Shadhdh* is the one which is reported by a trustworthy person while there is no one else to support this narration."Al-Hakim does not deem it necessary to be against the report of some more trustworthy reporters.

The following is a good example from among the *Ahadith* of Al-Hakim himself.

> *Isnad*: Al-Hakim reports through Ubaid b. Ghannam Al-Nakh'i through 'Ali b. Hakim through Sharik through 'Ata b. al-Sa'ib through Abu Al-Duha through Ibn 'Abbas.

> **Text:** In each Earth there is a Prophet like your Prophet, an Adam like Adam, a Nuh like Nuh, an Ibrahim like Ibrahim and an 'Isa like 'Isa.

Al-Hakim said: "This Hadith has a sound Isnad." Al-Baihaqi said: "The *isnad* is sound but it seems to be completely *shadhdh*." Here Baihaqi gives no

---

[121] *Taujih al-Nazar*, p 289.

reason for his verdict, but as a skilled traditonist he finds this Hadith at odds with the whole of Hadith literature.

According to the above two definitions, the Hadith of a single trustworthy reporter ranks as *shadhdh*. This is why al-Shafi'i's definition remains as the most acceptable. The opposite of *shadhdh* is known as *mahfuz*, and the opposite of *munkar* (an unreliable reporter narrating. something contrary to that of reliable reporters) is known as *ma'ruf.*

According to some traditionists, the Hadith of a single unreliable reporter (whether he goes against a reliable reporter or not) is to be held as *munkar.* For example, a Hadith transmitted by Nasa'i and lbn Majah:

> *Isnad*: Abu Zukair Yahya b. Muhammad b. Qais through Hisham b. 'Urwah through his father through A'isha.

> **Text:** The Prophet ﷺ said: "Eat Balah (fresh dates) with dry dates because it enrages the Satan whenever he sees it, and he says, 'The son of Adam lived until he ate the fresh with the old.'"

Nasa'i said: "This is a Munkar Hadith. Only Abu Zukair reported it. He is a good *shaykh*." Imam Muslim reported through him as a witness but he did not reach the level where his single report could be tolerated. Many Imams of Hadith see him as a weak authority. Ibn Ma'in said: "He is weak." Ibn Hibban said: "Not good for argument." 'Uqaili said: "No witness is found for his *Ahadith*." Ibn 'Adi said: "His *Ahadith* are good except for four, this one being among them."

9. The Knowledge of *al-Jarh wa 'l-Ta'dil* (Disparaging and Authenticating)

Under *'Rijal al-Hadith'*, a brief history of the traditionists concerned with the criticism of reporters has been given. Here we take it in detail.

The basis for this type of criticism is the saying of Allah:

$$\text{﴿ يَـٰٓأَيُّهَا ٱلَّذِينَ ءَامَنُوٓاْ إِن جَآءَكُمْ فَاسِقُۢ بِنَبَإٍ فَتَبَيَّنُوٓاْ أَن تُصِيبُواْ قَوْمَۢا بِجَهَٰلَةٍ فَتُصْبِحُواْ عَلَىٰ مَا فَعَلْتُمْ نَٰدِمِينَ ﴾}$$

"O you who have believed, if there comes to you a disobedient one with information, investigate, lest you harm a people out of ignorance and become, over what you have done, regretful." (Surah Al-Hujarat: 6)

Let us take the history of *al-Jarh wa 'l-Ta'dil* in chronological order.

a) During the time of the Prophet ﷺ

The Prophet ﷺ said: "Are you afraid of mentioning a sinful person? Mention him, so that the people could avoid him.'"[122]

Aisha said: "A man asked permission to enter upon the Prophet ﷺ. So he said, "Allow him. What a bad person from the tribe he is."[123]

Though backbiting is prohibited, this type of discussion falls under that which is allowed. It is allowed because of the dire need to protect the Hadith of the Prophet ﷺ from lies.

b) During the time of the Companions

Some examples of extreme care exercised by some *Sahaba* (like Aisha, Ibn 'Umar, 'Umar and 'Ali) have already been mentioned. Other Companions known with such concern are Abu Bakr, Zaid b. Thabit, Ibn Abbas, Abdullah b. Salam, Ubada, b. Al-Samit and Anas b. Malik.

c) During the time of the Successors

---

[122] *Al-Kifayah*: 88.
[123] Bukhari, *Kitab Al-Adab*, 13:81, Muslim 2: 551.

Among the most renowned Successors who spoke about the reporters are the following:

- Sa'id b. Al-Musayyab (d. 93 AH)
- Amir Al-Sha'bi (d. 104 AH): held to be a great scholar and the first one to scrutinize the Isnad.
- Ibrahim Al-Nakh'i.
- Al-Hasan Al-Basri (d. 110 AH)
- Tawus Al-Kaisan (d. 106 AH)
- Muhammad b. Sirin (d. 110 AH)
- Said b. Jubair (d. 94 AH)
- Muhammad b. Shihab Al-Zuhri (d. 124 AH)
- Ayyub As-Sikhtiani (d. 131 AH)

d) During the second half of the second century

A great number of traditionists were known with their opinions of the reporters, such as the following:

- Sulaiman b. Mihran Al-'A'mash (d. 148 AH)
- Ma'mar b. Rashid (d. 153 AH)
- Hisham Al-Dastawa'i (d. 154 AH)
- Al-Auza'i (d. 156 AH)
- Shu'ba b. Al-Hajjaj (d. 160 AH)
- Sufyan Al-Thauri (d. 161 AH)
- Abdul Aziz Al-Majishun (d. 164 AH)
- Hammad b. Salamah (d. 167 AH)
- Hammad b. Zaid (d. 175 AH)
- Al-Laith b. Sa'd (d. 175 AH)
- Malik b. Anas (d. 179 AH)
- Yahya b. Sa'id Al-Qattan (d. 189 AH)
- Abdul Rahman b. Mahdi (d. 198 AH)
- Abdullah b. Al-Mubarak (d. 181 AH)
- Abu Ishaq Al-Fazari (d. 185 AH)

- Waki' b. Al-Jarrah (d. 197 AH)
- Sufyan b. 'Uyaina (d. 198 AH)

e) During the first half of the third century

This period witnessed a great development in this field, during which persons like Yahya b. Ma'in and Ahmad b. Hanbal served the Sunnah, each in his own way. Yahya deleted the lies from the Hadith of the Prophet ﷺ and Ahmad stood firm during the trials to which he was subjected during the Abbasid period. He presented this Ummah with the biggest collection of Hadith. Now let us take the prominent ones known with authenticating and disparaging remarks:

- Abu Dawud Al-Tayalasi (d. 203 AH)
- Muhammad b. Idris At-Shafi'i (d. 204 AH)
- Yazid b Harun (d. 206 AH)
- Abu Asim Al-Nabil Makhlad (d. 211 AH)
- Abdul Razzaq b. Hammam (d. 211 AH)
- Muhammad b. Yusuf Al-Firyabi (d. 212 AH)
- Abu Bakr Abdullah b. Az-Zubair Al-Humaidi (d. 219 AH)
- Abu Abdallah b. Salama Al-Qa'nabi (d. 221 AH)
- Abu 'Ubaid Al-Qasim b. Salam (d. 224 AH)
- Yahya b. Yahya Al-Naisaburi ((i. 226 AH)
- Abul Walid Al-Tayalisi (d. 227 AH)
- Yahya b. Ma'in (d. 233 AH)
- Ali b. Al-Madini (d. 234AI-1)
- Ahmad ibn Hanbal (d. 241 AH)
- Abu Bakr Abdullah ibn Muhammad b. Abi Shaiba

These are known to be the first ones to write in this regard.

f) During the second half of the third Century

During this period six famous collectors of Hadith came to light. Among them Bukhari (d. 256 AH), Muslim b. Hajjaj (d. 261 AH), Abu Dawud (d. 275 AH), Tirmidhi (d. 279 AH), Al-Nasa'i (d. 303 AH) and Muhammad b. Yazid Ibn Maja Al-Qizwini (d. 251 AH) are known with their remarks about the reporters.

Also add to them:

- Abu Bakr Ahmad b. Zuhair b. Abi Khaithama (d. 279 AH)
- Abu Zur'a Abdul Rahman b. 'Amr (d. 281 AH)
- Abu Zur'a Abdullah b. Abdul Karim (d. 264 AH)
- Ibrahim b. Ya'qub Al Jauzajani (d. 259 AH)

g) During the later period until the tenth century

A lot of written material is added during this period. Note the names of some famous writers with their books under *Rijal al-Hadith* in our book *The Science of Hadith*.

We can safely say that this knowledge served the collectors of major books of Hadith in their quest to find out whether a Hadith was sound or not. Those *Ahadith* which escaped them, and were collected by later traditionists could be judged by the Books of *Rijal*, compiled during the remaining six centuries. There was not much to add to this knowledge by the end of the first millennium of the Islamic calendar. Authors like Muhammad b. Abdul Rahman Al-Sakhawi (d. 902 AH) and Jalal ul-Din Abdul Rahman Al-Suyuti (d. 911 AH) could only gather together the existing material or summarize it.

Books compiled on this subject are of three categories:

1. Those that mention reliable reporters only (*Kutub al-Thiqat*), e.g. *Tadhkirat ul-Huffaz* by Al-Dhahabi (d. 747 AH).

2. Those that mention weak and abandoned reporters (*Kutub al-Du'afa wal Matrukun*), e.g. *Ma'rifat al-Majruhin wa al-Du'afa* by Ibn Hibban (d. 354 AH).

3. Those which combine both types of reporters, e.g. *Kitab al-Jarh wa al-Ta'dil* by Ibn Abi Hatim Al-Razi (d. 327AH).

10. Anthenticating remarks

According to Ibn Hajar, the authenticating remarks are to be classified in the following six categories.

1st:

Authenticating words with superlative remarks like:

a)   *Awsaqul Nas* – أوثق الناس - Most trustworthy

b)   *Asbatul Nas* – اثبت الناس - Most solid

c)   *Adbatul Nas* - اضبط الناس - Best preserver

d)   *Ilaihi al-Muntaha fi al-Tathabbut* – إليه المنتهى في التثبت - He is the goal in establishing a Hadith

e)   *La Ahad Athbatu minhu* – لا أحد اثبت منه - None is more established than him

f)   *Man mithlu fulan* – من مثل فلان - Who could be like him?

2nd:

a)   *Thiqa, Thiqa* – ثقة ثقه - Trustworthy and reliable

b)   *Thiqa, Thabt* – ثقة ثبت - Trustworthy and solid

c)   *Thiqa, Mutqin* – ثقة متقن - Trustworthy and efficient

d)   *Thiqa, Hafiz* – ثقة حافظ - Trustworthy, Preserver

e)   *Thabt, Hafiz* – ثبت حافظ - Solid, Preserver

f)   *Thabt, Hujja* – ثبت حجة - Solid, an authority

3rd:

a) *Thiqa* - ثقة - Trustworthy

b) *Mutqin* - متقن - Efficient

c) *Thabt* - ثبت - Solid

d) *Hujja* - حجة - An authority

e) *Ka 'annahu Mushaf* – كأنه مصحف - As if he is a scripture

f) *Dabit* - ضابت - Preserver

g) *Imam* - إمام - Leader

h) *Hafiz* - حافظ - Preserver

4th:

a) *Saduq* - صدوق - Very truthful

b) *Ma'mun* - مأمون - Dependable

c) *Laisa bihi ba's* - ليس به بأس - Nothing wrong with him

d) *La ba'sa bihi* - لا بأس به - Nothing wrong with him

5th:

a) *Shaykh* - شيخ - Teacher

b) *Yurwa Hadithuhu* - يروي حديثه - His Hadith is to be narrated

c) *Shaikh Wasat* - شيخ وسط - Teacher of a middle level

d) *Salih ul Hadith* - صالح الحديث - Good at Hadith

e) *Yuktabu Hadithuhu* - يكتب حديثه - His Hadith is to be recorded

f) *Muqaribul Hadith* - مقارب الحديث - Near to the Hadith of others

g) *Saduq Sayyi'ul Hifdh* - صدوق سيء الحديث - Truthful but with bad memory

h) *Saduq Yahimu* - صدوق يهم - Truthful but speculates

i) *Saduq Lahu Auham* - صدوق له أوهام - Truthful but with many speculations

j) *Saduq Taghayyara bi Akhirihi* - صدوق تغير بأخره - Truthful but has changed in the end

6th:

a)   *Maqbul* - مقبول - Acceptable

b)   *Saduq Insha Allah* - صدوق ان شاء الله - Truthful by Allah's will

c)   *Arju an la ba'sa bihi* - أرجو أن لا بأس به - I hope that there is nothing wrong with him

d)   *Suwaileh* - صويلح - A little good

According to Ibn Hajar, reporters of the first four classes are acceptable in the transmission of Hadith while the last two classes are only good in the purpose of *i'tibar* (finding support and witnesses for a Hadith). Apart from those remarks, some traditionists also used detailed words of commendation, like: "He is like a mountain of knowledge", or "None is equal to him in my eyes".

11. Disparaging Remarks

Because of the sensitive nature of speaking ill about a person, the traditionists are found to be very careful in this matter. They agree that even if a person is known with many defects, the least should be mentioned about him.

Imam Malik said: "Knowledge is not taken from four types of People:

i.   The one who is known with stupidity, even if he is found to be a great narrator.

ii.   The one who generally speaks lies even though you do not accuse him of lying against the Prophet ﷺ.

iii.   A man of innovation who calls others to his innovation.

iv.   A Shaikh known with piety and worship, but does not know what he is narrating."[124]

They were also reluctant to take knowledge from these groups of people:

a) Innovators like Khawarij, Rawafid, Negators of Qadar, Murji'a, Batiniya and others.

b) Anyone found to be abusing the *Salaf* (the first generations of Islam like the *Sahaba* and the Successors).

c) Ambiguous persons; those who are not known in the circles of knowl edge, and no one reports from them except a single person.

d) Those who are known with lies.

e) Those who are known with *Tadlis*

f) Ascetics known with piety and worship but not with knowledge.

g) Story-tellers.

h) Those who are known with lots of mistakes.

i) Those who are found to be very relaxed in their narratives.

j) Those who are found to be confused either because of mental problems or because of turning senile.

According to Ibn Hajar, the reporters with disparaging remarks are also classified in six categories:

1st:

a)   Remarks with superlative degrees, e.g. 'the biggest liar'.

b)   He is the end in lying.

c)   A pillar of lies, or a mine of lies.

d)   A mountain of lies.

e)   A sock of lies.

---

[124] *Al-Jarh wa Al-Ta'dil* by Abu Lubaba Husain, p 93.

2nd:

a)   Dajjal (Imposter).

b)   A liar and an imposter.

c)   He fabricates.

d)   He lies.

3rd:

a)   He steals the Hadith (i.e. a traditionist is known with a particular Hadith, then a person comes along and claims that he has also heard this Hadith from the *shaykh* of that traditionist).

b)   Accused of lying and fabricating.

c)   Fallen out, left out (*Saqit, Matruk*).

d)   Perished (*Halik*).

e)   His Hadith is gone (*Dhahib ul Hadith*).

f)   They abandoned him.

g)   No regard is given to him.

h)   He is not trustworthy.

4th:

a)   His Hadith is rejectable.

b)   Very weak.

c)   Very fragile.

d)   They abandoned him completely.

e)   His Hadith is not to be recorded.

f)   Writing his Hadith is not allowed.

g)   Repeating from him is not allowed.

h)   He is nothing.

5th:

a)   He is not good for the sake of argument.

b)   They held him as weak.

c)   Shaky in Hadith.

d)   Denounced.

e)   He has rejected in Hadith.

f)   Weak.

6th:

a)   There are sayings about him.

b)   At least, something is said about him.

c)   Weakness is found in him.

d)   Denounced some times, recognized some other times.

e)   He is not like those!

f)   He is neither strong nor solid.

g)   He is not an authority or a pillar.

h)   He is not dependable or trustworthy.

i)   He is not agreeable.

j)   They do not praise him.

k)   He is not a preserver of Hadith.

l)   Others are more trustworthy than him.

m) Something is in him.

n)   Ambiguity is in him.

o)   I do not know who he is.

p)   Weakness is in him.

q)   A person with bad memory.

r)   Lenient in Hadith.

s)   In him is leniency.

t)   They spoke about him.

u)   They kept quiet about him.

v)   He is to be looked at.

The reporters in the first four categories are to be rejected completely. The last two categories are good for I'tibar but they are still inferior in rank when compared, to the last two groups among those who were listed under "Authenticating remarks."

12. What about a person who attracted both Authenticating and Disparaging Remarks?

It is quite possible to have opposite remarks about a reporter from two different traditionists. The question to be asked is: What type of remarks should be given preference? For example, Imam Abu Hanifa said about Ja'far al-Ju'fi: "I have not seen a person a bigger liar than Ja'far al-Ju'fi." However, Waki' said about him: "Were it not for Ja'far al-Ju'fi, the people of Kufa would have been without Hadith."[125]

There are three opinions advanced regarding this issue:

i.   *Ta'dil* (integrity) of a person is the basis. It is to be preferred against any type of *Tarjih* (disparaging).

ii.   *Tajrih* means an additional knowledge with the criticiser. So it should be given preference.

iii.   *Tajrih* is to be given preference if it is given in detail, as traditionists differ in their criteria regarding the causes by which a person is disparaged. They may be acceptable, they may be not. For example, al-Hakam b. 'Utbah did not report from Zazan because he talked too much (*Al-Kifaya*: 183). Shu'ba abandoned a person because he saw him galloping on the back of a mule. (*Al-Kifaya*: 182). And this is why Bukhari did report from Ikrima, the free slave of Ibn 'Abbas, even though he was criticized by some. Ibn Hajar made the matter clearer by saying that if an Imam from among the traditionists has authenticated a person, no *Tajrih* could be accepted about

---

[125] *Kitab al-Ilal* by Tirmidhi, 5:741.

him unless it was given in detail, i,c. the reason behind this *Tajrih* is given. But, if the reporter does not carry such a commending certificate, undetailed disparaging remarks would be enough to discredit.[126]

There are a number of regulatory principles that have been laid down by the traditionists in order to acccept *Tajrih* right from the beginning. Let us take these principles briefly:

1. A criticiser should be just in passing his remarks. Besides *Tajrih*, he should not forget mentioning the good side of a person if there was something to say. For example, Ahmad b. Hanbal said about Abu Ma'shar al-Sindi, a historian: "He has a place in knowledge and history. Imams have taken from his history book but held him weak in Hadith."

Abdullah b. Al-Mubarak used to commend 'Abbad b. Kathir al-Thaqafi because of his religious ways, but also warned the people regarding taking Hadith from him.[127]

2. Every criticism motivated by jealousy or hatred is rejected. Ibn 'Abbas said: "Listen to the knowledge of the scholars but do not believe one against the other because they are more jealous to each other than the rams in their herds."[128]

Such remarks are a common phenomenon among the contemporaries. For example, that of Muhammad ibn Ishaq (the historian) who said about Imam Malik: "Present to me the knowledge of Malik as I am a doctor (to judge it)." To this Malik replied: "Look at this big imposter who claims to scrutinize the knowledge of Malik."[129]

---

[126] *Tadrib al-Rawi*, 1:308.
[127] *Sahih Muslim, Al-Muqaddima* 1:17.
[128] *Jami Bayan al-'Ilm* by Ibn Abdil Barr, 2: 158.
[129] *Al-Maghazi Al-Ula wa Mu'allifuha*, p 79.

3. Criticism based on the affiliation to a different school of thought is also rejected. For example, the criticism of As-Subki (d. 771 AH) against his own Shaikh al-Dhahabi (d. 748 AH), because of the latter's opinion about Asha'ira.[130]

4. Criticism of ascetics against scholars because of their involvement in worldly affairs is not acccpted. For example, Makhul used to condemn Al-Zuhri because he had close relations with the rulers.[131]

5. Criticism of a traditionist known with very hard views would not be accepted about a reporter if no one else shared his views, like those of Yahya b-Ma'in, Yahya b. Sa'id Al-Qattan and Ibn Hibban. It is noted that a reporter abandoned by Ibn Al-Qattan may still be accepted by Abdullah b. Al-Mubarak, Waki' b. AI-Jarrah and Abdul Rahman b. Mahdi.[132]

6. As for the ten types of people as mentioned in the previous (11th) section, the Hadith of some of them may be accepted if certain conditions are met. For example:

a. Innovators: A distinction is made between the one who calls towards his innovation and the one who does not. The latter is to be accepted while the former is to be rejected.

b. Ambiguous reporters: Ambiguity is lifted if the scholars commend the reporter or at least two reliable persons are found to report his Hadith.

c. Mudallis: Their reports are not acccpted except for those who were found to be practising Tadlis through reliable authorities like that of Sufyan b. 'Uyaina.[133]

d. Reporters with lots of mistakes: They could only be accepted if their narratives come through other sources as well.

---

[130] *Qa'ida fil Jarh wa al-Ta'dil* by Al-Luknawi, p 14.
[131] *Al-Maghzi Al-Ula,* p 62.
[132] *'Ilal* by Al-Tirmidhi.
[133] *Sahih Ibn Hibban,* 1: 122.

e. Those confused in their old age: Whatever they reported before confusion is acceptable, as opposed to those narratives which they reported after confusion. Imam Ahmad said about Al-Mas'udi: "Waki' and Abu Nu'aim both reported from Mas'udi at Kufa. Confusion happened to him when he moved to Baghdad. Anyone who listened to him at Kufa or Basra, there is nothing wrong with him."[134]

13. The Methods through which knowledge is carried

Here follows a summary of the chapter entitled *Tahammul Al-'Ilm: Carrying of Knowledge of Ahadith* from M. M. Azmi's book *Studies in Hadith Methodology and Literature*.

Learning of Hadith in early days

For learning of Hadith the following eight methods were used:

1. *Sama'*: that is reading by the teacher to the students.
2. *'Ard*: reading by students to teachers.
3. *Ijazah*: to permit someone to transmit a Hadith or book on the authority of the scholar without reading by any one.
4. *Munawalah*: to hand someone the written material to transmit it.
5. *Kitabah*: to write Ahadith for someone.
6. *I'lam*: to inform someone that the informer has permission to transmit certain material.
7. *Wasiyah*: to entrust someone his books.
8. *Wijadah*: to find some books or Ahadith written by someone just as nowadays we discover some manuscripts in a library or somewhere else.

____

[134] *Ilal* by Ahmad, 1:95.

But, in the period of the Companions, only the first of these methods was in general use, while the use of other methods was negligible. A man was not entitled to use any Hadith in his literary life if he had not received it by one of the eight above mentioned ways that is up to number seven. Number eight was not recognized by the scholars. Now we shall discuss these methods in some detail.

1. *Sama'* (سماع): Reading by the teacher to the students

This method has the following features: Oral recitation, reading from books, questions and answers, and dictation.

Oral recitation of Ahadith by the teacher: Usually, the students were attached to a certain teacher for a very long time, until they were believed to be authorities on the Ahadith of their teachers. Sometimes they were called Rawi or Sahib of so and so.

Reading from books: Reading by the teacher, from his own book, which was preferred.

Dictating the *Ahadith*: This method was not encouraged in the early days because in this way a student could gather much knowledge in a very short time without much effort. It seems that al-Zuhri was the first to depart from this attitude. About the end of the first century we find him dictating *Ahadith*, a method which he followed during the rest of his life.

2. `*Ard* (عرض): Reading to teachers

Another method was that the book was read by the students to the teacher or by a certain man called a Qari, or other students compared Ahadith with their books or only listened attentively. Later they copied froin the books. This method was called 'Ard.

3. *Ijazah* (إجازة) Permission

In Hadith terminology Ijazah means to permit someone to transmit a Hadith or book on the authority of a certain scholar who gave this permission, without having read the book to him. There have been different kinds of Ijazah. Until the third century, it is difficult to find signs of the Ijazah system, but it was widely used later. There have been differences of opinions about its validity.

4. *Munawala* (مناوله): Handing the books to a student

When someone gave a student a manuscript along with the authority to transmit it. For example Zuhri gave his manuscripts to several scholars, like Thauri, Auza'i and Ubaidullah b. Umar. It was called Munawala. This was not a common practice in the early days.

5. *Kitabah* (كتابه): Correspondence

This means writing Ahadith to give them to someone else to transmit. There were quite a good deal of activities of this sort. This practice started from very early days and can be assumed to have started from the very beginning. Official letters ofthe rightly guided Caliphs contained many Ahadith which were transmitted by scholars. Besides this many companions and later on many scholars wrote down Ahadith and sent them to their Students. See for example lbn 'Abbas's writings to lbn Abu Mulaikah and Najdah.

6. *I'lam* (أعلام): To inform about Ahadith

I'lam meant to inform someone that informer has permission to transmit a certain book on certain scholars' authority. Some of the scholars permitted this method of transmitting Ahadith while others rejected it. The only benefit from it was that the second person had to find the original copy which bore the certificate and the name of the person who gave permission. Signs of this method are difficult to trace in the early period,

7. *Wasiyah* (وصية)

To entrust someone the book which may be transmitted on the authority of the one who entrusted the books. For example Abu Qilabah (d. 104 AH) who entrusted his books to Ayyub al¬-Sakhtiyani.

8. *Wijadah* (وجادة)

That is to find someone's book without any sort of permission to transmit on anyone's authority. This was not a recognized way of learning Ahadith. According to the standard of the Muhaddithin one must State explicitly that the information he presented had been taken from the book of such a man. There are references to books of this sort from very early days. An example is the book of Sa'd b. Ubadah (d. 15 AH),

Terms used to describe transmission of Ahadith

There are many terms employed by Muhaddithun for this purpose. As every Isnad contains many names therefore these terms are repeated frequently. To save space and time Muhaddithun used abbreviations or, say, a short-hand method for this purpose, and even used to drop some word from Isnad. These are the terms:

- *Haddathana* (حدثنا) mostly, written *Thana* or *Na* only.
- *Akhbarana* (أخبرنا) mostly written *Ana* only and rarely *Arana*.
- *Haddathana* (حدثنا) is used mostly to denote learning through the reading by the teacher (1st method).
- *Akhbarana* (أخبرنا) is used to denote learning through the second method, though some of the scholars used these two terms interchangeably.
- *Anba'na* (أنبأنا) is used in *Ijazah* and *Munawala*, and sometimes even *Haddathana Ijazatan* is used in *Munawala*.
- *Sami'ah* (سمع) is used in the learning through the first method only.

- *'An* (ﻋﻦ) can be used in all the methods.

All these terms are not of equal value. *Sami'tu, Haddathana, Haddathani, Akhbarana* and *Akhbarani* are the most superior, though the authorities differ about which is best among them. However, *'An'* is very inferior.

These terms should not be changed in copying. *'An'* is not explicit for direct contact between narrators, therefore in the case of a narrator who was accused of practising *Tadlis*, it might cause the Hadith to be judged a weak one.

PART TWO

A) CLASSIFICATION OF HADITH IN ACCORDANCE WITH THE ATTRIBUTES OF THE REPORTERS

1. *Al-Sabiq wa al-Lahiq* السابق والاحق (The foremost and the runner up)

Among the reporters from a certain *shaykh*, the knowledge of the first ones (*Al-Sabiq*) and the last ones (*Al-Lahiq*) helps to reach a higher *isnad* (with less medium between a reporter and the Prophet ﷺ in comparison to a lower Isnad with more mediums). It further alleviates any doubt about the possibility of interruption between these two reporters.

For example, from Shaikh Muhammad b. Ishaq Al-Sarraj (d. 256 AH), two prominent persons have reported; Imam Bukhari (d. 256 AH) and Ahmad ibn Muhammad Al-Khaffaf (d. 395AH). The difference between the death dates of both is about one hundred and thirty-nine years.[135]

2. The knowledge of brothers and sisters among the reporters

This knowledge helps to alleviate any doubt about the relation between two reporters who happen to have a common name as far as their fathers are concerned, but have no filial relation. For example, Abdullah b. Dinar is not a brother of 'Amr b. Dinar because their fathers are different though they have a common name. Take a few examples of real brothers among the Companions:

---

[135] *Mu'jam Istilahat e Hadith* by Dr Suhail Hasan, p 191.

- Abdullah b. Mas'ud and Utba b. Masud
- Zaid b. Thabit and Yazid b. Thabit
- 'Amr b. Al-As and Hisham b. Al-As
- Ali, 'Aqil and Ja'far, sons of Abu Talib

Among the Successors, we find Muhammad b. Sirin reporting from his brother Yahya who reports from their third brother Anas.[136]

3. *Al-Muhmal* المهمل (Unknown) and *al-Mubham* المبهم (Obscure)

Muhmal: If the two names are found to be common and there is nothing to suggest a distinction between the two of them.

For example, Imam Bukhari reports from two persons both named as Ahmad. He could be Ahmad b. Salih or Ahmad b. 'Isa. Anyhow, both are trustworthy. Similarly there are two persons with the names of Sulaiman b. Dawud. One of them with the attribution of Khaulani is trustworthy while the other, known as Yamani, is weak.[137]

Mubham: That reporter whose name is not mentioned in an *isnad*. The Hadith narrated by such a reporter is unacceptable unless he is identified.[138]

The difference between *muhmal* and *mubham* is that the *isnad* of *muhmal* is not affected if both reporters are found to be trustworthy. However, it is certainly affected if one of them is found to be weak, primarily because you do not know who is who in that particular Isnad. As for *mubham*, the man is not identified. As long as his integrity is unknown, his Hadith is not acceptable.

---

[136] *Taysir Uloom al-Hadith* by Mahmud al-Tahhan, p 188.
[137] *Al-Mu'jam Mustalahat al-Hadith* by Dr Diya al-Rahman Al-Azami, p 509.
[138] *Taysir*, p 111.

4. *Al-Musalsal* المسلسل (Uniformly linked)

See the detailed section in the book above *An Introduction to the Science of Hadith*.

5. *Al-Muttafiq wa 'l-Muftariq* المتفق والمفترق (Common names with different identities)

There are many examples of common names, not only of the reporters themselves but of their fathers and grandfathers, of their affiliation to certain towns and localities.

For example, there are six persons by the name of Khalil b. Ahmad. They are only distinguished because of either their nicknames or their attribution. They are:

- Khalil b. Ahmad Al-Isfahani
- Khalil b. Ahmad Al-Sijizzi
- Khalil b. Ahmad Abu Sa'id Al-Busti Al-Qadi
- Khalil b. Ahmad Abu Sa'id Al-Busti Al-Shafi'i

Al-Khatib Al-Baglidadi has cited in his book 'Al-Muttafiq wa Al-Muftariq' an amazing example, of 'Abdullah b. Al-Harith, a name shared by seventeen reporters.

By this knowledge, one can avoid linking two or more reporters to just one identity. It also helps to rank a Hadith either as sound or weak in accordance to the credibility of the reporter.[139]

---

[139] *Al-Mu'jam*, p 344.

6. *Al-Mu'talif wa 'l-Mukhtalif* المؤتلف والمختلف (Similar but pronounced differently)

This knowledge belongs mainly to the shape of the words in a name. They are of three types:

i.   Similarity in word, different in pronunciation like سلام (*Salam*) and سلام (*Sallam*) and مسور (*Miswar*) and مسور (*Musawwar*).

ii.   Looks alike in writing but there is a difference of lettering, like حزام (*Hizam*) and حرام (*Haram*), حيان (*Hayyan*) and حبان (*Hibban*)

iii.   Similar in writing but different in *Tashkil* (i.e. *Fatha, Kasra, Dhamma, Sukun* on each letter) like حصين (*Husayyin*) and حصين (*Hasin*).

This knowledge helps a reader to avoid changes and interpolation.[140]

7. *Al-Mutashabih* المتشابه (Symmetrical)

See No. 35, Section C of *An Introduction to the Science of Hadith*.

A further branch of this type is *al-Mutashabih al-Maqlub* (Symmetrical but inverted), like Aswad b. Yazid and Yazid b. Aswad. The second name is turned over to the first name.[141]

---

[140] *Ibid*, p 334.
[141] *Ibid*, p 340.

8. *Al-Muharraf* المحرف (Interpolated) and *al-Musahhaf* المصحف (Distorted)

The first one comes out of *tahrif* (Interpolation). The words in writing remain the same, but the meaning is totally changed because of a different reading of the same word. For example:

نهى النبي ﷺ عن الحلق قبل الصلاة يوم الجمعة

The word under discussion is الحلق, the plural of حلق meaning 'group'

Thus the Hadith means: "The Prophet ﷺ forbade grouping before the Friday prayer".

But, someone taking it as الحلق (to shave) has changed the meaning totally.

The second term is derived from *tashif* (distortion) which is done in two ways:

i. To change the word in writing, like أحتجم (He cupped: suckling out the spoilt blood by way of the method of cupping), which is changed to أحتجر (He corifined himself to a room).
    A second example is that of this Hadith:

    من صام رمضان واتعه ستاً من شوال كأنه صام الدهر كله

    "Whoever fasts the month of Ramadan and follows it with six days (fasting) of Shawwal, is like a person who fasts throughout his life."

    The word ستاً was changed by some reporters to شيئاً meaning 'something'.

ii. The reporter did not change the word but misunderstood it. For example, it is reported in a Hadith:

    ان النبي ﷺ صلى إلى العنزة

    "The Prophet ﷺ prayed towards an 'Anaza": a stick with a sharp end dug into the ground for the purpose of Sutrah.

But the tribe of Banu 'Unaiza took this word as a mention of them, so they proudly said that the Prophet ﷺ has prayed facing the direction of their tribe.[142]

B) CLASSIFICATION OF HADITH IN ACCORDANCE WITH THE AGE GROUP OF THE REPORTERS

1. The narratives of *al-Aqran* الأقران (Contemporaries) and *Mudabbaj* مدبج (Beautified)

If a person reports from another similar to him in age or in his *isnad*, his report comes under this heading, e.g. Sulaiman At-Taimi reporting from Mis'ar b. Kidam.

If they report from each other, such a report is known as Mudabbaj (Beautified), like that of 'Aisha and Abu Huraira from among the Companions, Zuhri and 'Umar b. 'Abdul Aziz from among the Successors, Imam Malik, and Awza'i from among the Successors to the Successors, and Imam Ahmad and Ali b. Al-Madini from those after them. This knowledge helps to avoid any doubt about an addition in Isnad.[143]

2. Fathers reporting from sons

Among the examples are:

i. 'Abbas b. Abdul Muttalib reports from his son Fadl that the Prophet ﷺ prayed Maghrib and Isha combined in Muzdalifah.

ii. Among the Successors, Wa'il reported from his son Bakr about eight Ahadith.

---

[142] *Ibid*, p 98.
[143] *Taysir,* p 164.

iii.   Abu 'Umar Hafs b. 'Umar Al-Dauri reported sixteen Ahadith from his son Abu Ja'far Muhammad b. Hafs.

This knowledge alleviates any doubt about Isnad; whether or not it has been overturned, because a son normally reports from his father.[144]

3. Sons reporting from their fathers

i.   A son is known for reporting solely from his father, like Abul 'Ushara (Usama b. Malik) who only reports from his father Malik.

ii.   The *isnad* consists of three generations or more where a son reports from his father who reports from the grandfather. A famous example is that of ' Amr b. Shu'aib -- his father - his grandfather. This *isnad* needs clarification.

   The family line of 'Amr is like this: `Amr b. Shu'aib b. Muhammad b. Abdullah b. 'Amr b. Al-As. 'Amr reports from his father Shuaib. Shu'aib reports from his own grandfather (Abdullah, the son of the famous Companion 'Amr b. Al-As), and not from his own father (Muhammad, the grandson of 'Amr). A similar example is that of Bahz b. Hakim - his father - his grandfather.[145]

This knowledge helps to find out the identity of fathers and grandfathers, whose names may have been missed by the reporters.

---

[144] *Mu'jam* by Suhail Hasan, p 49.
[145] *Muqaddima* by Ibn Salah, p 540.

4. Elders reporting from their juniors.

Under this heading such reporters are mentioned who are found to be:

i. Elder and higher in rank than those from whom they have reported, like Imam Zuhri and Yahya b. Sa'id Al-Ansari reporting from Imam Malik.

ii. More knowledgeable and famous than their Shaikh, like Imam Malik reporting from Abdullah b. Dinar.

iii. Elder and more famous than their Shaikh, like Burqani reporting from Khatib al-Baghdadi.

This knowledge helps to eradicate this notion that a Shaikh is always older in age and more reputable than his pupil and that there might have been a change in *isnad*.[146]

5. The knowledge of the life history of the reporters

It is very important to know the dates of birth and death of every reporter in order to establish the continuity of *isnad*. Someone may claim that he heard such and such person (among his Shuyukh) but it may not be true if that *shaykh* happened to die before the birth of the reporter himself.

For example 'Isma'il b. 'Ayyash confronted a reporter who claimed to have heard from Khalid b. Ma'dan by asking him, "When did you hear from him?" He said "In the year 113 AH." Isma'il said: "So you claim that you have heard from Khalid seven years after his death?" as Khalid died In 106 AH.[147]

---

[146] *Al-Mu'jam* by Azami, p 164.
[147] *Al-Taqyid wa al-Idah* by Al-Iraqi, p 432.

C) THE MANNERS REQUIRED IN TRADITIONISTS AND THEIR STUDENTS

a) The manners required by the seekers of knowledge:

i. To seek the knowledge within sincerity of intention, looking for the pleasure of Allah alone.

ii. His objective should not be to gain some worldly benefits, but he should seek his knowledge as a form of worship.

iii. He should try to act upon Ahadith that come to his knowledge.

iv. He should always look for help from Allah and keep on praying to Him for assistance in the course of his pursuit of knowledge.

v. He should devote himself comletely towards seeking the knowledge.

vi. He should begin his pursuit to hear Hadith from the Shuyukh of his own town, those who are known with knowledge and piety.

vii. He should respect his Shaikh. Respecting him is honouring the knowledge. He should always look for the pleasure of his Shuyukh, and should behave patiently even if treated badly.

viii. He should always inform his colleagues of any scholarly points that come to his knowledge.

ix. No shyness should stop him from seeking knowledge or hearing Ahadith. Similarly, advanced age or arrogance should also not be a hindrance for him.

x. He should not confine himself to listening to Ahadith or reading them, but they should be studied with somebody else.

xi. Preference should be given to learn and understand both *Sahih Books* (*Bukhari* and *Muslim*), *Sunan Abu Dawud*, *Tirmidhi* and *Nasa'i* come after them. Then come Baihaqi's *Al-Sunan Al-Kubra* and other *Masanid* and *Jawami'* like *Musnad*

Ahmad and *Muwatta'* of Imam Malik. The following books in the Science of Hadith should always be consulted:

- *'Ilal* of Daraqutni in the knowledge of hidden defects.
- *Al-Tarikh Al-Kabir* by Bukhari and Kitab al-Jarh wa al-Ta'dil by Ibn Abi Hatim as far as the reporters of Hadith are concerned.
- *Kitab al-Ikmal* by Ibn Makula about the accuracy of the names.
- *Al-Nihaya* of Ibn Al-Athir in knowing the odd and difficult words of Hadith.[148]

b) Manners required in a traditionist:

i. He should be sincere in his intention, away from material gains and worldly fame.

ii. His only objective should be to disseminate the sayings of tile Prophet ﷺ.

iii. In the presence of a more exalted or elderly scholar, he should not present himself for saying the Hadith.

iv. He should not hesitate to direct the students to someone else who happened to have acquired a particular Hadith when he is asked about it by his students.

v. He should read each word of the Ahadith clearly, and precisely, so that the students grasp them and can write them easily.

vi. He should always state the ruling about a weak Hadith if he happens to narrate it.

vii. He should not bar anyone from writing Hadith.

viii. He should always take into account the mental level of his audience when narrating Ahadith. He should not report such sayings that they fail to perceive or understand.

---

[148] *Al-Mu'jam* by Azami, p 24.

ix.   He should not confine himself to simply narrating Ahadith, but should try his best to explain the issues contained in order to avoid practising Ahadith which are either abrogated or found to be odd or impracticable.

x.   In the present circumstances, a person should not narrate Ahadith but after getting permission (*ijazah*) from his Shuyukh and after acquiring enough skill to differentiate between sound and weak Ahadith.[149]

c) Manners related to the court (*majlis*) of narrating Hadith

i.   He should attend the *majlis* after cleaning and purifying himself. Wearing perfume and combing the beard and head is also recommended.

ii.   Respect, honour and dignity should always be maintained in the *majlis*.

iii.   He should take care of all his audience, and must not concentrate on some particular individual.

iv.   He should begin his lesson by glorifying the name of Allah and offering praise and blessings to the Prophet ﷺ. He should supplicate according to the situation in the beginning and the end.[150]

---

[149] *Ibid,* p 24-26.
[150] *Taysir,* p 164

.

D) CLASSIFICATION OF HADITH AS RELATED TO THE IDENTITY OF THE REPORTERS[151]

1. The knowledge of obscure reporters (*Mubham*) مبهم

The definition of obscure reporters has already been given.

For example: Muslim transmitted in his Sahih that a man asked the Prophet ﷺ about Hajj, 'Is it a duty once every year?" This man, as mentioned in another narration, is Al-Aqra' b. Habis Al-Tamimi.

Both Bukhari aud Muslim reported on the authority of Anas that the Prophet ﷺ noticed a rope being tied between two pillars of the Mosque. When he inquired about it, he was told that this belonged to a woman who took hold of it whenever she became tired whilst standing for the prayer. She is recognized as either Umm ul-Mu'minin Zainab bint Jahsh or her sister Hamna, or Maimuna bint al-Harith.

This type of knowledge helps to:

- Find out the prestigious position of the person if the Hadith speaks good about him, or alleviate any doubt around his personality if something bad is mentioned.
- Once the name of the reporter is identified, it helps to find out if the Hadith is abrogated or not.

2. The knowledge of single reports (*al-Wuhdan*) الوحدان

Under this heading, such Shuyukh are listed from whom only a single person reports.

---

[151] *Al-Mu'jam,* p 337.

- Al-Musayyab b. Hazan: only his son Sa'id reports from him (both are Companions).
- Mu'awiya b. Haida: his son is the only one to report from him.
- Qurrah b. Iyas: his son Mu'awiya is the only one to report from him.
- Among the Successors, Abul 'Ushara Al-Darimi: only Muhammad b. Salamah reports from him.
- Among the Successors to the Successors, Miswar b. Rifa'a Al-Qurazi: only Imam Malik reports from him.

By this knowledge, ambiguous reporters come to light and except for the Companions, their reports are not acceptable.

3. The knowledge of reporters with different names, as well as such names which are either unique in their structure or are single ones from among the reporters

This knowledge helps to eradicate any doubt about a single person turned into many personalities. It also shuts the door towards Tadlis of Shuyukh. It also helps to eliminate any possibility of changes and interpolation in the reporters' names, nicknames and bynames.

Among the unique names are:

- Ahmad b. Ujayyan (Companion)
- Sundar (Companion)
- Ausat b. 'Amr
- Darib b. Naqir b. Samir.[152]

Some names are unique as there is no one else among the Sahaba and Tabi'in with the same name.

---

[152] *Muqaddima*, 562.

- Sham'un, Abu Raihana (Companion)
- Shakal b. Humaid (Companion)
- Zirr b. Hubaish (Successor)
- Al-Ma'rur b. Suwaid (Successor)
- Huzayyin b. Al-Mundhir (Successor)
- Muhammad b. al-Sa'ib al-Kalbi is known as Hammad as well. He is also known with two nicknames, Abul Nadr and Abu Sa'id.

4. Unique nicknames (Kunya)

Like Abul Hamra, Hilal b. al-Harith, the free slave of the Prophet ﷺ.

A particular knowledge of nicknames is essential to establish the identity of the reporter. This knowledge includes the following:

- A person known with his nickname: e.g. Abu Bilal Al-'Ashari (he had no other name), and Abu Nawas (It is not known whether he had another name or not).
- Persons known with their names and more than one nickname: e.g. 'Ali b. Abi Talib. His nicknames are Abul Hasan and Abu Turab (the second is a byname as well), lbn Juraij: he has two nicknames, Abul Walid and Abu Khalid.
- A person with a difference of opinion about his nickname: e.g. 'Usama b. Zaid: He is either Abu Muhammad or Abu Abdullah, or Abu Kharijah.
- A person known with his nickname, although there is a difference of opinion about his name: e.g. Abu Huraira, many opinions are given about his name and his father's name. The most famous opinion is that he is Abdul Rahman b. Sakhr.
- A person whose name and nickname are both disputed: e.g. Safina, the Companion. He is either 'Umar, or Sahh, or Mihran. His nickname is either Abu Abdul Rahman or Abul Bukhari.

- A person famous with both his name and nickname: e.g. Sufyan Al-Thauri, Malik, Al-Shafi'i and Ahmad b. Hanhal: all are known with the nickname of Abu Abdullah. Imam Abu Hanifa is known more with his Kunya than his name Nu'man b. Thabit.

- A person who is well known with his Kunya, though his name is also known: e.g. Abu Idris Al-Khaulani, His name is 'Aidhullah.

- A person who is well known by his name while his Kunya is also known: e.g. Talha b. 'Ubaidullah Al-Taimi, Abdul Rahman b. Awf and Hasan b. Ali b. Abi Talib. All of them have the Kunya of Abu Muhammad.[153]

5. The knowledge of bynames or titles (*Alqab*)

- Unique titles: e.g. Safina: his name is Mihran.
- Titles indicating a defect:
    - e.g. *Al-Dall* (الضـال) given to Mu'awiya b. Abdul Karim as he was lost on his way to Makka.
    - *Al-Da'if* (الضـعيف) a title given to Abdullah b. Muhammad because of his weak stature.
    - *Ghundur* (غندر) a title given to Muhammad b. Ja'far Al-Basri by Ibn Juraij because Ibn Ja'far made a noise in his class when he cattle to Basra.
- Some similar titles are:
    - *Al-A'raj* (الأعرج) meaning 'lame',
    - *Al-A'mash* (الأعمش) meaning 'bleary-eyed',
    - *Al-A'war* (الأعور) meaning 'one-eyed',
    - *Al-Bakkar* (البكار) meaning 'cries a lot'.
- Titles indicating commendable qualities: e. g.

---

[153] *Taysir,* p 199.

Ghunjar (غنجار) meaning "reddish cheek": two traditionists are known with this title, 'Isa b. Musa Abu Ahmad Al-Bukhari and Abu Abdullah Muhammad b. Ahmad Al-Bukhari.

Bindar (بندار) meaning "buying a lot then selling it": a title given to Muhammad b. Bashar al-Misri.

Mushkadana (مشكدانه) meaning "small box of musk", a title given to Abdullah b. 'Umar b. Muhammad Al-'Amawi.

- Some famous titles which were given to the Companions because of a reason, e.g.
    o *Dhul Yadain* (ذو اليدين): 'A person with two hands', a title given to a Companion who asked the Prophet ﷺ when he forgot in his prayer.
    o *Dhul Ghurra* (ذو الغره) 'A person with a shining forehead', a title given to Bara b. Azib.
    o *Dhul Shahadatain* (ذو الشهادتين) 'A person with two testimonies', a title given to Khuzaima b. Thabit.
    o *Dhul Nurain* (ذو النورين) 'A person with two lights', a title given to 'Uthman b. Affan.
    o *Dhul Udhunain* (ذو الأذنين): 'A person with two ears', a title given to Anas b. Malik.

6. Those attributed to other than their fathers

Some reporters are found to be attributed to others than their own fathers. This knowledge is important in order to avoid confusion if they are attributed - in some Asanid - to their fathers. Let us take some examples:

- Attributed to their mothers:
    o Mu'adh and Mu'awwadh, the sons of 'Afra bint 'Ubaid. Their father is Harith b. Rifa'a Al-Ansari.

- o Abdullah b. Umm Maktum (the *Mu'adhdhin* of the Prophet ﷺ)
  - o Suhail, Sahl and Safwan: all sons of Baida.
  - o Shurahbil b. Hasanah.
  - o Abdullah b. Buhainah.
  - o Isma'il b. 'Ulayyah.
  - o Sa'd b. Hiba.
- Attributed to their grandmothers:
  - o Ya'la b. Munya.
  - o Bashir b. Al-Khasasiya
  - o Imam lbnTaymiyya (She was his great grandmother)
- Attributed to their grandfathers. Once, during the battle of Hunain, the Prophet ﷺ attributed himself to his grandfather by saying:

أنا النبي لا كذب، أنا ابن عبد المطلب

"I am the Prophet without a doubt, I am the son of Abdul Muttallib."

- o Abu 'Ubaidah b. Al-Jarrah: His name is Amir and his father is Abdullah.
  - o Ibn Juraij: He is Abdul Malik b. Abdul Aziz b. Juraij.
  - o Mujamma' b. Jariyah
  - o Ibn Al-Majishun
  - o Ahmad b. Hanbal
- Attributed to a totally unrelated person:
  - o e.g. Miqdad b. 'Amr al-Kindi. He is also known as Miqdad b. al-Aswad (his stepfather).
  - o Hasan b. Wasil, known as Ibn Dinar (his stepfather)[154]

---

[154] *Al-Mu'jam,* p 461.

7. Attribution contrary to what it seems to be

Normally a reporter is attributed to his tribe, his hometown, his profession etc. However, sometimes they are attributed to something else. Traditionists have explained such attributes in order to avoid any confusion. For example:

- Abu Mas'ud 'Uqba b. 'Amr al-Badri: He is attributed to Badr, not because of participating in the battle of Badr, but because he stayed there for a while.
- Sulaiman b. Tarkhan Al-Taimi: He did not belong to Banu Taim but stayed there for a while.
- Yazid al-Faqir: Not because of *Faqr* (poverty) but because of an injury in his *Faqar* (part of the backbone).
- Khalid b. Mihran Abul Manazil Al-Hadhdha: Not because he was a shoemaker but because used to sit in their company.[155]

E) THE KNOWLEDGE OF TABAQAT (GROUPS) OF THE REPORTERS

By Tabaqat, we mean a certain group of people who share something in common. On top of the list come the Companions, who come in twelve groups as classified by Imam Hakim. Then come the Successors.

According to Ibn Hajar, the narrators of Hadith, especially those mentioned in the six books of Hadith, are classified in the following twelve groups:

1. The Companions.
2. Elder Successors, like Sa'id b. Al-Musayyab.
3. Successors of a middle rank like Hasan Al-Basri and Ibn Sirin.

---

[155] Ibid, p 463.

4. Those very near to those above them, who normally narrate from elder Successors, like Zuhri and Qatada.

5. Younger Successors, who have seen one or two Companions but they did not hear from them, like Al-A'mash.

6. Contemporary to the above group, but have not seen any Companions at all.

7. The elder Successors to the Successors, like Imam Malik and Thauri.

8. Those of middle rank from among them, 'like Ibn Uyaina and Ibn 'Ulayya.

9. Those younger from among them, like Yazid b. Harun and Imam Shafi'i.

10. Elder traditionists from those who reported from the previous group, like Imam Ahmad.

11. The middle ranks of such traditionists like Iniam Zuhli and Imam Bukhari.

12. Those younger from among them, like Imam Tirmidhi.[156]

F) THE KNOWLEDGE OF *MAWALI* موالي (PL. *MAULA*)

Though the term Maula is used for both the master and the slave, it is also used for a free slave. In Hadith terminology it applies to the following:

- A free slave who is attributed to the master that freed him, like Thauban, Shaqran, Ruwaifi', Zaid b. Haritha, Safina and Mihran. All were freed by the Prophet ﷺ and thus attributed to him.

- *Maula* meaning an ally like Imain Malik b. Anas Al-Asbahi Al-Taimi. He is 'Asbahi' because of his tribe and 'Taimi' because his grandfather Malik b. Abi Amir made an alliance with Banu Taim.

---

[156] *Taqrib Al-Tadhib* by Ibn Hajar: *Al-Muqaddimah*, p 75.

- *Maula* because of accepting Islam, For example, Imam Muhammad b. Isma'il al-Bukhari al-Ju'fi, Bukhari's grandfather was a magian who became Muslim on the hand of Yaman b. Akhnas al-Ju'fi. This is why he was attributed to him.

- *Maula* because of long company. For example, Miqsam *maula* Ibn Abbas. He was attributed to Ibn Abbas because he always lived with him though he is in fact a *Maula* of Abdullah b. Harith b. Naufal.

This type of knowledge helps to identify the real attribution of a person, which comes through *Muwalat* and not through a direct relationship.

G) THE KNOWLEDGE RELATED TO THE HOMETOWNS OF THE REPORTERS

A person is either attributed to his hometown, country or place where he resided for most of his life. This knowledge helps to identify a person if he is confused with another one because of a common name.

A person may have more than one place to which he is attributed. A later attribution can be added by inserting the word ثُمَّ (*Thumma* = then) between two places, for example, *Makki (thumma) Al-Basri*.

H) THE KNOWLEDGE OF *MUKHADRAM* مخضرم

This term is given to a person who lived in both periods: *Jahiliyya* (pre-Islamic era) and Islam, but he either accepted Islam after the death of the Prophet ﷺ, or he did not meet him though he became Muslim during the Prophet's ﷺ lifetime. They are treated like Successors. Iraqi has mentioned forty names from among this type of people. Some are listed below:

- Abu Muslim Al-Khaulani
- Abdullah b. 'Ukaim AI-Juhani
- Al-Ahnaf b. Qais Al-Tamimi, d. 67 AH
- Al-Aswad b. Yazid Al-Nakh'I, d. 74 AH
- Aslam Maula 'Umar, d. 80 AH
- Uwais b. Amir al-Qarni
- Shuraih h. Al-Harith Al-Qadi, d. 80 AH
- Abdul Rahman b. Ghunm, d. 78 AH
- Qais b. Abi Hazim Al-Bajali
- Masruq b. Al-Ajda' Al-Hamdani, d. 62 AH[157]

I) THE KNOWLEDGE OF TRUSTWORTHY REPORTERS WHO WERE HELD AS WEAK

There is no doubt that a sound Hadith depends entirely on trustworthy reporters, but there may be some reliable reporters who were held as weak due to a temporary phase of life or any other reason. Once that reason disappears, his credibility is restored.

Such repotters are classified in three categories:

i) Those who were held as weak in a certain phase of their lives (e. g. during the confusion of old age), like 'Ata b. Al-Sa'ib, Husain b. Abdul Rahman Al-Sulami, Sa'id b. Abi 'Aruba.

ii) Those who are held weak for a specific reason, like Ma'mar b. Rashid. He is reliable when he reports from the Shuyukb of Yemen, but held weak when he reports from those of Basra.

Imam Ahmad says about Abdul Razzaq b. Hamman Al-Sam'ani that his reporting from Sufiyan at Makkah is questionable.

---

[157] *Al-Taqyid wal 'Idah* by 'Iraqi, p 281.

Isma'il b- 'Ayyash Al-Himsi is reliable in his reports from the people of Sham. (Sy'ria), but is otherwise unreliable.

Zuhair b. Muhammad Al-Khurasani: whatever the people of Iraq report from him is acceptable, unlike what is reported from the people of Sham from him.

iii) Such reporters who are reliable by themselves, but whose Shuyukh are not reliable like Hammad b. Salama, who is a trustworthy reporter but there is a lot of confusion in the reports of some of his Shuyukh.[158]

J) THE KNOWLEDGE OF THE REPORTERS OF THE SIX BOOKS

A lot of interest is shown by the traditionists towards the reporters of the six major collections of Hadith (i.e, Bukhari, Muslim, Tirmidhi, Nasa'i, Abu Dawud, Ibn Majah). Many books have been compiled about their life-sketches, listing the name of the *shuyukh* and pupils alike, along with authenticating and disparaging remarks about them.

Some of the most important works are listed below:

- *Al-Kamal fi Asma al-Rijal* by Al-Hafiz Abdul Ghani b. Abdul Wahid Al-Maqdisi (d. 600 AH).
- *Tahzib Al-Kamal fi Asma al-Rijal* by Al-Hafiz Jamaluddin Al-Mizzi (d. 742 AH). It is a summary of the first book with many additions to it.
- Five books, all summarizing *Kamal* by Al-Dhahabi (d. 748 AH), with the titles of *Tadhhib, Al-Kashif, Al-Mujarrad, Al-Muqtadab* and *Mizan al-l'tidal.*

---

[158] *Al-Mu'jam,* p 107.

- *Al-Takmil fil Jarh wa al-Ta'dil* by Ibn Kathir (d. 774 AH), It combines the contents of Mizzi's *Tahzib* and Dhahabi's *Mizan.*
- Two books of Ibn Hajar (d. 852 AH) by the names of *Tahdhib al-Tahdhib* and *Taqrib al-Tahdhib.* The last one is very popular with students of Hadith as it is a concise version of *Al-Kamal.*
- Yet another short and summarized version of *Al-Kamal,* which gained much popularity as well, is *Khulasa Taddhib Tahdhib Al-Kamal* by Al-Hafiz Safiyuddin Al-Khazraji Al-Ansari (d. 923 AH).[159]

K) OTHER BRANCHES OF KNOWLEDGE

1. Gharib al-Hadith

The knowledge of explaining difficult words in Hadith literature

2. Mushkil al-Hadith

The knowledge of seemingly contradictory Ahadith and how to reconcile among them

3. Al-Nasikh wal Mansukh

The knowledge of abrogated Ahadith and of those that abrogate them

4. Asbab Wurud al-Hadith

The knowledgc of the circumstances behind the Prophet's (SAS) savings or actions

---

[159] *Mu'jam* by Dr Suhail Hasan, p 75-76.

MY PERSONAL IJAZAH

The reader would be pleased to know that the tradition of *isnad* has been preserved until this day.

I myself have received *ijaza* of Hadith from my father, Shaikh Abdul Ghaffar Hasan (May Allah protect him). His *isnad* goes back to the Prophet (SAS) through twenty three *shuyukh*, via his Shaikh Ahmadullah (d. 1362 AH), from Syed Nadhir Husain Al-Dehlawi (d. 1320 AH), and through twenty-five *shuyukh* through Muhammad b. Ali Al-Shaukani (d. 1250 AH) of Yemen.

Both *asanid* pass through eminent *shuyukh* like:

- Shah Waliullah Al-Dehlawi (d. 1176 AH)
- Ahmad b. Ali b. Hajar Al-Asqalani (d. 852 AH)
- Abdul Rahim b. Husain Al-Iraqi (d. 806 AH)
- Muhammad b. Isma'il Al-Bukhari (d. 256 AH)
- Muhammad b. Abdullah Al-Ansari (d. 215 AH)
- Humaid al-Tawil b. Abi Humaid (d. 143 AH)
- Anas b. Malik (the Companion d. 93 AH)

LIST OF HADITH TERMINOLOGY

Some of the terms are given a new equivalent in English as opposed to what is recorded in the *Science of Hadith*.

مرفوع Elevated

موقوف Suspended

مقطوع Severed

مسند Supported

متصل Continuous

منقطع Broken

معلق Hanging

معضل Perplexing

مرسل Incompletely transmitted

متواتر Recurrent

آحاد Isolated

غريب Rare

عزيز Strong

مشهور Well known

شاذ Odd

منكر Denounced

مدرج Partly added

معلل Defective

مقلوب Inverted

مضطرب Shaky

صحيح Sound

حسن Good

ضعيف Weak

موضوع Fabricated Forged

عدالة Integrity

علة Defect

مبهم Obscure

مصحف Distorted

محرف Interpolated

ضبط Preservation

مدلس Hidden

متروك Discarded

معروف Celebrated

مهمل Unknown

مسلسل Uniformly linked

www.ingramcontent.com/pod-product-compliance
Lightning Source LLC
Chambersburg PA
CBHW021221130726
47988CB00002B/757